Leadership Development Basics

Karen Lawson

ASTD
PRESS

Alexandria, Virginia

ASTD Press is an internationally renowned source of insightful and practical information on workplace learning and performance topics, including training basics, evaluation and return-on-investment, instructional systems development, e-learning, leadership, and career development.

Ordering information: Books published by ASTD Press can be purchased by visiting our website at store.astd.org or by calling 800.628.2783 or 703.683.8100.

Library of Congress Control Number: 2007941493

ISBN-10: 1-56286-535-8
ISBN-13: 978-1-56286-535-1

ASTD Press Editorial Staff:
Director: Cat Russo
Manager, Acquisitions and Author Relations: Mark Morrow
Editorial Manager: Jacqueline Edlund-Braun
Senior Associate Editor: Tora Estep
Associate Editor: Maureen Soyars

Copyeditor: April Davis
Indexer: April Davis
Proofreader: Kris Patenaude
Interior Design and Production: PerfecType, Nashville, TN
Cover Design: Elizabeth Park
Cover Illustration: Rob Colvin, www.images.com

Printed by Victor Graphics, Inc., Baltimore, Maryland, www.victorgraphics.com.

Contents

About the
Training Basics Series

ASTD's *Training Basics* series recognizes and, in some ways, celebrates the fast-paced, ever-changing reality of organizations today. Jobs, roles, and expectations change quickly. One day you might be a network administrator or a process line manager, and the next day you might be asked to train 50 employees in basic computer skills or to instruct line workers in quality processes.

Where do you turn for help? The ASTD *Training Basics* series is designed to be your one-stop solution. The series takes a minimalist approach to your learning curve dilemma and presents only the information you need to be successful. Each book in the series guides you through key aspects of training: giving presentations, making the transition to the role of trainer, designing and delivering training, and evaluating training. The books in the series also include some advanced skills such as performance and basic business proficiencies.

The ASTD *Training Basics* series is the perfect tool for training and performance professionals looking for easy-to-understand materials that will prepare non-trainers to take on a training role. In addition, this series is the perfect reference tool for any trainer's bookshelf and a quick way to hone your existing skills.

Preface

■■

The need for good leadership has never been greater, and there is no doubt we are experiencing a leadership deficit throughout our society—corporations, governments, and communities. Almost daily, we are bombarded by articles in newspapers and professional publications bemoaning the lack of qualified leaders to meet the challenges of a diverse workforce, global competition, and an uncertain economy.

To meet the growing demands for qualified leaders, organizations are choosing to grow their leaders from within rather than hiring from the outside. To that end, organizations are identifying high-potential employees who have qualities, skills, and abilities that are aligned with corporate values and leadership philosophy and then giving them the training, coaching, and experiences they need to help the organizations succeed. Interestingly, most organizations do not have a well-defined process in place to develop the next generation of leaders. In many cases, the approach to leadership development is a combination of "baptism by fire" and "trial and error." Training and other development activities take place independently of each other, resulting in a hodgepodge of experiences without focus or clearly defined goals and outcomes.

Who Should Read This Book

This book provides a broad overview of the elements and the process for implementing a leadership development program in your organization. It serves as a starting point to help you understand what is involved in undertaking an integrated, comprehensive approach to developing your leadership pipeline. Readers who will benefit from this book include

> ▶ chief learning officers and other learning leaders
> ▶ organization development professionals

▶ human resource professionals
▶ senior management and other leaders.

Leadership Development Basics provides the tools and techniques needed to design, develop, and implement a leadership development program in your organizations. Readers will be able to choose the program components appropriate to their organizations based on corporate strategies and goals, size of the organization, and available resources (financial as well as human capital).

Look for These Icons

This book strives to make it easy for you to understand and apply its lessons. The following icons used throughout this book will help you zoom in on key points.

What's Inside This Chapter?

Each chapter opens with a summary of the topics in the chapter. You can use this reference to find the areas that interest you most.

Think About This

These are helpful tips for how to use the tools and techniques presented in the chapter.

Basic Rules

These rules cut to the chase. They represent important concepts and assumptions that form the foundation of a leadership development program.

Noted

This icon calls out additional information.

Getting It Done

The final section of each chapter offers suggestions, additional resources, or questions that will help you implement a leadership development program in your organization.

The Need for Leadership Development

What's Inside This Chapter

In this chapter, you'll learn

▶ The conditions and trends driving leadership development
▶ The importance of leadership development
▶ Shifts in leadership behaviors and expectations
▶ Leadership competencies.

Over the last five years, there has been an increased emphasis on leadership development. Why? Corporate America is in a crisis mode. As a result, organizations are waking up and realizing that they must invest in leadership development. Although a leadership development program may be costly, it is well worth the investment. Companies with strong leadership bench strength will outperform the competition and exceed business goals. Organizations that fail to do so will operate in a crisis mode, scrambling to find replacements when critical positions become vacant.

Noted

The Society for Human Resource Management's 2005 Future of the U.S. Labor Pool Survey Report *found that, of the 263 companies surveyed, 45 percent were just becoming aware of the issues posed by the retirement of baby boomers.*

Trends Driving Leadership Development

Let's take a look at some of the business and social trends that are driving the need for leadership development.

Retiring Baby Boomers

More than 70 million baby boomers (born between 1946 and 1964) will retire between 2008 and 2023, and, during this time, only 40 million people will enter the workforce. Massive retirements of baby boomers will result in talent shortage, knowledge drain, and leadership gaps especially at the top levels that are currently filled by baby boomers. Also lost will be personal internal and external networks that are vital to getting things done as well as a loss of historical context.

Think About This

It can take up to 10 years to develop critical expert knowledge that leaves with a retiring employee.

—*Dorothy Leonard and Walter C. Swap in* Deep Smarts: How to Cultivate and Transfer Enduring Business Wisdom

Downsizing and Mergers

The belt-tightening of the 1990s resulting in massive layoffs wiped out layers of middle management and depleted the talent pool. During those years, management development programs fell by the wayside. Consequently, there are simply not enough managers to meet the demand. Lack of ready-now executive talent is increasing the importance of developing internal candidates to fill key leadership positions.

Globalizing

Without doubt the world is shrinking. As more and more companies do business internationally, the emphasis on developing leaders who can help their companies succeed in a global environment will increase. Even domestic companies need to have a global mindset because the company will more likely buy or sell abroad. At the very least, a U.S.-based organization will be influenced by global events and the global economy.

Changing Workforce

Twenty-first century employees are different. They demand to be more involved in decisions that affect them, and they require a different kind of leader, one who will solicit their ideas, listen to them, and provide coaching and feedback on a regular basis.

Losing Employee Loyalty

Starting with Gen Xers (born between 1965 and 1977) and increasing with Gen Yers (born after 1978) who are now entering the workforce, job hopping has become the norm. Many of those who are now in their twenties and thirties observed their baby boomer parents give their all to a company, often sacrificing precious family time, only to be shown the door after 25 or 30 years of loyal service.

Changing Structures

Organizations have changed from top-down, hierarchical structures to flatter, more streamlined operations with decentralized business units and virtual offices. As companies become more team-oriented and collaborative, fewer opportunities exist to develop leaders as the traditional leadership pipeline presents fewer candidates from which to choose.

Lacking Accountability

There is a lack of accountability for developing employees. Although executives have given lip service to the importance of leadership development, they have not put any substance behind the pronouncements. In most companies, managers not only are not rewarded for developing their employees, but also receive no negative consequences for not developing their employees.

Changing Technology

Rapidly changing technology presents both opportunities and challenges. On the plus side, organizations can get things done quickly and efficiently. Leaders can stay connected to and communicate with their employees regardless of location or time zone. On the minus side, technological advances create an increasingly complex environment, one in which people are required to do more with less, putting even more strain on already limited resources.

Importance of Leadership Development

All these factors have created a renewed interest in the importance of leadership development as a key business strategy. There is finally a recognition that organizations need to develop better leaders more quickly.

The professional development of managers, department heads, and executives is critical to the efficient operation and success of any organization. Meeting the continuous learning needs of managers at all levels in a fast-paced, demanding, and changing environment is the key to maintaining a competitive advantage. The ability to develop an innovative, comprehensive, and integrated leadership development program will lead to overall increased organizational effectiveness and a firm foundation for developing future executives and building a quality-driven leadership team. Although leadership development in corporations is on the increase, most companies do a poor job of developing their managers and executives. Studies show that poor succession planning and poor leadership development often result in high-potential managers leaving the organization for better growth opportunities. Recent survey results indicate that inadequate succession planning and leadership training are the most critical leadership development issues in organizations today.

Unfortunately, many companies that do invest in leadership development still fall short in their efforts to prepare the next wave of leaders for the rapidly changing business climate. Many programs are still designed as a series of events rather than as a system or process that supports an overall development strategy. Forward-thinking companies are taking an integrated approach to leadership development by incorporating other programs and initiatives such as mentoring, coaching, job rotation, performance management, and succession planning. Furthermore, these innovative and visionary companies recognize that leadership development must be aligned with the organization's business strategy.

The need for superior leadership talent has never been greater, and yet companies are finding it increasingly more difficult to attract and retain top performers. Because this situation is not likely to improve in the foreseeable future, it is imperative that organizations identify and develop their leadership talent from within.

Noted

A Corporate Leadership Council survey found that approximately three-fourths of companies worldwide are not confident in their ability to effectively staff leadership positions over the next five years.

—Jeff Snipes in "Identifying and Cultivating High-Potential Employees," CLO

Shifts in Leadership Behaviors and Expectations

Today's leaders and managers face tougher challenges than ever before. Cultivating an environment in which people thrive requires new insights and skill sets for effective leadership. The old ways of doing business don't work anymore. Managers must go beyond traditional managerial roles and functions. They must now be leaders, charged with the responsibility of influencing others to go the extra mile to achieve organizational goals.

Today's employees and business conditions require a different type of leader. Successful leaders are those who reflect the following shifts in thinking and behavior.

Collaborating, Not Competing

Although organizations will continue to stress competition in the world marketplace, effective leaders will demonstrate a more collaborative style both inside and outside the corporate environment. They will break down internal silos by reaching across traditional business-unit dividing lines to work on joint projects, develop new products and services, share resources, and solve business problems. They will also form partnerships with other organizations, even their competition, to expand their influence and increase market share. The pharmaceutical industry is a good example of companies that have joined forces to launch new products. This type of collaborative style needs to be fostered at every level of leadership.

Empowering, Not Evaluating

Effective leaders will create an environment that fosters the desire and ability of employees to make decisions and take action without first asking permission. Employees will be encouraged to take ownership of their work and responsibility for their results. This type of environment will enable leaders to spend more time engaged in broad-based thinking, visioning, and developing their employees.

Being Proactive, Not Reactive

Being proactive involves both strategic and critical thinking skills. It requires leaders to be innovative and take risks, to take the initiative in developing new processes and tools to outperform the competition. It also involves the ability to look at and understand both the immediate and the long-term consequences of each decision and action and to identify challenges and opportunities inherent in both existing and future trends.

Listening, Not Telling

Rather than doing most of the talking, true leaders will spend more time asking questions and then really listening to employees. The key is to ask the right questions to help people find the best solutions themselves. Effective leaders will hold frequent one-on-one and group meetings to ask questions and listen to concerns and get to know their employees on a more personal basis. They will conduct stay interviews designed to find out what people want from their jobs and what motivates them to stay with the organizations. They actively solicit ideas and suggestions from their employees and are open to new ways of doing things even if it opposes existing viewpoints and practices.

Coaching, Not Directing

Traditional leaders often issue directives, expect people to follow them without question, and then penalize them when they don't quite meet expectations. Today's leaders will use coaching skills to help people improve their performance to either close a performance gap or help them go above and beyond and achieve their personal best.

Leadership Competencies

The first step in establishing a leadership development program is to identify organization-specific leadership competencies. Leadership competencies are the personal and professional attributes and skills critical to successful performance and organizational effectiveness. These competencies must be both observable and measurable. Since 2000, there have been countless studies on leadership competencies. For example, a 2006 study conducted by Right Management Consultants identified the most desired management and leadership abilities for future executives:

- ▶ motivate and engage others—62 percent
- ▶ communicate effectively, strategically, and interpersonally—58 percent
- ▶ think strategically—52 percent
- ▶ lead change—51 percent
- ▶ create a performance organization—47 percent.

In reviewing and comparing results from a number of studies, the following emerged as the core competencies of effective leaders:

- ▶ building relationships
- ▶ communicating and influencing
- ▶ adapting to changing circumstances
- ▶ using emotional intelligence
- ▶ motivating and inspiring employees
- ▶ supporting teams
- ▶ setting or sharing a vision
- ▶ coaching and developing employees
- ▶ having self-awareness
- ▶ having honesty, integrity, and ethics
- ▶ managing change
- ▶ focusing on the customer
- ▶ solving problems and making decisions.

Before organizations can even begin to address the required leadership competencies, they need to create an organizational context. They must first identify the business strategy and then determine the competencies needed to execute that strategy. Once this has taken place, the organization can begin to develop its leadership development program, making sure the leadership competencies are tied to the corporate values and desired business outcomes.

The logical next step is to equip the organizations' leaders with the behaviors, knowledge, and skills to be more effective in serving their employees, customers, communities, and stakeholders. This is accomplished by providing a comprehensive and structured leadership development program consisting of competency-based learning modules and other activities related directly to developing specific leadership attributes and skills.

A critical element of a successful program is accountability. The participants in the leadership development program must be held accountable for applying what they learned in the program and demonstrating that they are ready, willing, and able to truly lead the organization in a positive direction.

The need to create pools of candidates with high leadership potential has never been greater. Although a leadership development program may be costly and time-consuming, it is well worth the investment. Companies with strong leadership bench strength will outperform the competition and exceed business goals.

Basic Rule 1
Organizations must create strong leadership bench strength.

Getting It Done
To identify the level of commitment for a leadership development program, conduct one-on-one meetings with key decisions makers in the organization and ask them the following questions:

1. What is your vision for a leadership development program?
2. What is the reason you want to implement a leadership development program at this time?
3. What is your leadership philosophy?
4. How has the leadership philosophy in this organization changed over the past five years?

In the next chapter, you will explore the concepts of leadership development and how leadership development supports the organization's strategic plan.

2

Filling the Need: Leadership Development Programs

 What's Inside This Chapter

In this chapter, you'll learn

▶ The definition of leadership development
▶ The relationship of leadership development to the strategic plan
▶ Objectives and benefits of a leadership development program
▶ Critical components of a leadership development program.

As noted in chapter 1, a gap in the leadership pipeline is a critical and growing challenge for organizations. Although the need for leadership talent is increasing, many organizations have not responded accordingly. Often the reason for inaction is not lack of desire but rather lack of understanding as to what leadership development is and how to do it. Leadership development has many definitions and can take many forms ranging from a casual ad hoc approach to a highly structured, multifaceted formal program.

Leadership Development Defined

For our purposes, leadership development is a strategic investment in a structured process that provides individuals with the opportunities, training, and experiences to become effective leaders in their organizations. It is an integrated approach to developing their knowledge and skills to enable themselves and their organizations to succeed. Leadership is no longer confined to those with titles. Today, leadership applies to everyone throughout the organization regardless of rank, title, position, or job grade, and an organization's leadership pipeline must start with people who are not leaders yet.

Basic Rule 2

Leadership can be learned by creating leadership opportunities and using those experiences as teaching points.

Creating an Organizational Context

Before implementing any program, it is important that those responsible for such implementation create a context in which leaders can be successful. The first place to start is to look at the organization's strategic plan. Leadership development at all levels must be linked directly to the strategic objectives and challenges facing the organization.

Developing a Strategic Plan

Strategic planning is a process in which leaders of the organization imagine a pre-ferred future and develop the processes, procedures, and operations that will enable them to achieve this future.

The strategic plan itself is the written analysis, objectives, goals, and steps that explain how an organization chooses to carry out its mission and fulfill its vision. For a strategic plan to have any value, implementation and follow-up also need to be part of the process. A strategic plan should have the following elements.

Vision

A vision is a wish or dream about how leaders would ideally like the organization to be; it is the preferred future. A vision is inspirational.

Mission

A mission statement describes the purpose of an organization or a sub-group of it. It is a general description of what it is that the group is there to do. It grows out of the vision. It describes the purpose of the organization, what the organization does, for whom the organization works, and in what manner the organization works. It tends to be general, which then requires the accomplishment of many specific goals. The mission statement provides the broad framework for goals and objectives. It also provides guidance for the major decisions officers and managers need to make.

A mission statement is a concise summary of an organization's reason for existence that everyone can understand and remember. It should be a single sentence of no more than 25 to 30 words.

Values

Values are the collective set of deeply ingrained beliefs, ethics, and priorities that guide organizational and individual behavior. An organization's values should guide the identification, selection, training, and development of leaders at all levels.

Goals

Goals are more specific than the mission, may have a short or long timeframe in which they are carried out, may change over the years to reflect changes in need or demand for products or services, and provide the framework within which objectives can be set and measured.

Objectives

Objectives are most specific in scope. They are statements of outcome that describe certain conditions that must be met within a specified timeframe. Objectives may change within a short timeframe. They are measurable and expressed in quantities.

SWOT Analysis

SWOT is an acronym for strengths, weaknesses, opportunities, and threats. These categories of information are traditional bases for determining strategy.

Strengths—An organization's internal capabilities or resources (within and largely controlled by the organization) that are better than those of its competitors. They are areas of value in the organization and among the organization's stakeholders.

Weaknesses—An organization's internal capabilities or resources (within and largely controlled by the organization) that are worse than those of its competitors.

Opportunities—Circumstances, usually outside an organization, that have potential benefit for the organization and provide the organization with the chance to explore new directions. They are positive influences over which the organization has no control.

Threats—Circumstances, usually outside an organization, that could harm the organization; they represent potential dangers that could prevent or inhibit the future success. They are negative influences over which the organization has no control.

Critical Success Factors

Critical success factors are the few high-priority areas the organization must manage to be successful. They are the characteristics, conditions, and variables that, when properly maintained and managed, can most positively affect an organization's success. Some examples are as follows:

▶ maintain financial performance that relates favorably to peer or industry norms

▶ develop and maintain high-quality sales and service programs and systems

▶ provide profitable, quality services designed to meet customer needs

▶ establish measurable and attainable growth goals and targets

▶ ensure compliance with applicable regulatory and legal issues

▶ strengthen and promote corporate image in the community.

Critical success factors also apply to the competencies of high-potential employees. Examples include versatility, flexibility, and initiative.

Determining Leadership Competencies

Once the organization is clear about its strategic direction, including its vision, mission, and values, the next step is to identify the leadership competencies needed to take the organization where it wants to go. The business strategy must drive the competency model, and the competencies must be tied to the desired business outcomes. How do you determine the desired competencies? You first determine the business requirements that will in turn determine the leadership competencies. Then you determine the business challenges and competencies needed to meet those challenges. The identification of leadership competencies should be part of the strategic planning process, and one of the best ways to approach the process of identifying leadership competencies is to revisit the SWOT analysis that was part of the strategic plan.

If the organization's top leaders do not want to reinvent the wheel, numerous studies have identified many examples of leadership competencies. The most common examples are listed in chapter 1. However, just identifying the desired competencies is not enough. It is critical that they be further refined by defining them in performance-based behavioral terms followed by "so that" and then stating the benefits or outcomes. Let's take a look at the following example:

Competency: Leading Change

Behavioral Description: The ability to lead and manage change within the organization and help others cope with and manage change (behavior) **so that** the organization can respond rapidly and effectively to a changing business environment (benefit/outcome).

By stating the competency in behavioral terms, everyone is clear as to what is expected as well as the business reason for it. It is also a starting point for identifying the metrics or other indicators to measure the competency. You also have a consistent set of criteria on which to base selection, development, and leadership assessment. It also ensures strong strategic alignment and consistent behavior among leaders at all levels. Although senior leaders will ultimately make the decision on the competencies as well as critical success factors, they should first seek input from other leaders at various levels throughout the organization.

Once the competencies have been determined and clearly communicated and embraced throughout the organization, the logical next step is to equip the organization's leaders with the behaviors, knowledge, and skills to be more effective in serving their clients and employees. This is accomplished by providing a comprehensive and structured leadership development program consisting of competency-based learning modules.

Basic Rule 3
Developing a leadership infrastructure will attract and retain top talent and can position companies for future success.

Objectives and Benefits of a Leadership Development Program

First and foremost, a leadership development program must focus on business results. It must have an integrated approach with a strategic focus that addresses key business challenges.

A successful leadership development program must change and adjust to the new competitive environment. It must be both company focused and industry specific.

Finally, comprehensive leadership development communicates vision, values, and strategy throughout the organization.

 Basic Rule 4
Leadership development is a process, not a series of events.

The implementation of a well-designed, integrated leadership development program will result in tangible benefits for the organization. A successful program will enable the company to

▶ develop better leaders
Managers will develop a strategic and more global perspective. They learn how to become transformational rather than transactional leaders.

▶ create a talent pool
A leadership development program will help create a pool of leadership talent as well as a cadre of executives who can implement strategy and get results.

▶ preserve corporate culture
Participants begin to identify themselves with the organization. They embrace wholeheartedly the organization's vision, mission, values, and goals and are committed to creating and maintaining a dynamic, supportive, and team-oriented culture.

▶ attract and retain talent.
Successful organizations attract successful people. Organizations that value

human capital recognize that investing in high-potential managers is the key to maintaining a competitive advantage in the marketplace.

Noted

Issues of leadership are changing at all levels within organizations. According to the SHRM 2006 Talent Management Survey Report, *talent management initiatives are a top priority in businesses.*

Leadership Development Practices

"Leader Machines," an article in *Fortune* by G. Colvin (2007), identified nine practices shared by those ranked as the "Top Companies for Leaders":

1. *Invest time and money.* In addition to allocating the necessary financial resources, all leaders from the CEO on down must promote and participate in leadership development programs.

2. *Identify promising leaders early.* Due to increasing labor shortages, companies must assess potential leaders earlier in their careers than has been the practice in the past. There simply are not enough Gen Xers available to take the place of retiring baby boomers.

3. *Choose assignments strategically.* Effective leadership development programs must employ a variety of methods, assignments, and activities that are targeted to individual development needs and linked closely to the long-term, as well as the short-term, needs of the organization. These experiences must be chosen carefully to challenge individuals and force them out of their comfort zones so they can really stretch and grow.

4. *Develop leaders within their current jobs.* To counteract turnover and maintain stability within the department or business unit, leaders will need opportunities to take on short-term assignments and participate in activities in addition to their current job responsibilities.

5. *Be passionate about feedback and support.* Frequent, honest feedback coupled with a lot of support through coaching and mentoring must become part of everyday practice at all levels in the organization.

6. *Develop teams, not just individuals.* To support and learn from each other, leaders should be put into learning teams to attend training events and work on group assignments.

7. *Exert leadership through inspiration.* Leadership is about creating an environment in which people are not only motivated but also fully engaged in their work. Effective leaders know the difference between compliance and commitment, and they use influencing behaviors to get employees to do what the leaders want them to do because the employees genuinely want to do it.

8. *Encourage leaders to be active in their communities.* When leaders get involved in their communities they have a greater understanding of the relationship between their organizations and the communities in which they work. Progressive organizations not only encourage their leaders to be actively involved in their communities, but also give them time off to do so.

9. *Make leadership development part of the culture.* Leadership development becomes a part of all organization decisions, practices, processes, and objectives. Furthermore, learning leaders are seen as trusted advisers and strategic partners who help integrate leadership development into all aspects of the organization.

Think About This

As one who is (or will be) instrumental in driving the successful implementation of a leadership development program, you need to influence others to support the leadership development initiative and focus on building relationships throughout the organization.

Critical Components of a Leadership Development Program

A successful leadership development program doesn't just happen. It must be planned very carefully and reflect the following components:

1. The top leaders of the organization must demonstrate a strong commitment to the program.
2. The program must be linked to the vision, values, and strategies of the organization.

3. The program must be tied to succession planning.

4. The program must meet both individual and organizational needs.

5. Leadership competencies must be clearly identified, defined, and communicated throughout the organization.

6. There must be a developmental assessment related to the leadership competencies.

7. Individual development plans must be part of a leader's performance objectives.

8. Leaders at all levels must be involved in teaching and coaching.

9. Educational activities must be linked to organizational and business issues.

10. Senior management must monitor the program.

 ## Getting It Done

To help prepare your organization for a comprehensive leadership development initiative, complete the Organizational Readiness Checklist in table 2-1 and then ask the key leaders in your organization to do the same.

Table 2-1. Organizational Readiness Checklist.

Use the following checklist to determine how ready your organization is to implement a leadership development program.

	Yes	No
The organization truly values its employees.	❏	❏
Senior management has clearly identified and communicated the organization's vision, mission, and values to all employees.	❏	❏
Some management development or supervisory skills programs are in place.	❏	❏
The organization has a structured performance management system that focuses on pay for performance.	❏	❏
Employees are encouraged to take advantage of educational and developmental opportunities.	❏	❏

continued on next page

Table 2-1. Organizational Readiness Checklist (continued).

Managers are involved in coaching and giving feedback to their employees.	❏	❏
Managers encourage feedback from those they supervise.	❏	❏
Performance standards are in place and are clearly communicated to employees.	❏	❏
Employees are encouraged to be proactive and take risks.	❏	❏
Senior management is willing to allocate the necessary resources (time, money, people) to ensure a successful leadership development program.	❏	❏

Compare the responses. Note which items show a discrepancy in responses, then meet with all those involved to discuss their perceptions, the reasons for their responses, and identify any actions that need to be taken before you design the leadership development program.

In the next chapter, you will learn about the first step in creating a leadership development program, the development of a comprehensive succession management system that reaches beyond the C-suite-level positions and includes leaders at all levels.

3

Preparing Tomorrow's Leaders Today

■ ■

What's Inside This Chapter

In this chapter, you'll learn

▶ How leadership development is tied to succession planning
▶ What high potential means
▶ Various assessment methods and tools
▶ How to create a leadership development plan.

Organizations cannot afford to wait until the need arises to begin developing their leaders. The process of preparing tomorrow's leaders should be incorporated into and be driven by the succession plan and the corporate goals and strategies. Unfortunately, many organizations don't even have a succession plan.

Succession Planning

What is succession planning, and why is it important? Simply put, succession planning is a systematic process of developing individuals to fill key roles in the organization. The purpose of a succession planning program is to ensure continuity of leadership and the smooth operation of the organization by matching the goals and needs of the organization to those of the individual. A good succession plan ensures the continued smooth operation of the organization by developing internal candidates for leadership positions at all levels. It enables an organization to identify and prepare the right people for the right position at the needed time. Furthermore, succession planning enables the organization to maintain a competitive advantage, fosters a positive climate of growth and development, maintains leadership continuity, and ensures the best use of human resources to achieve individual growth and organizational success. Without a succession plan, organizations will find themselves continually operating in a crisis mode, scrambling to find replacements when critical positions become vacant.

Succession planning can take several forms. Simple replacement planning, as the name implies, is a process that indicates possible internal replacements for critical positions and may involve formal developmental plans or activities. In many cases, the individual identified may just be the next in line by virtue of tenure or position. Developmental succession planning indicates possible internal replacements but also involves specific developmental activities for the express purpose of grooming them for higher level responsibilities and positions. Finally, the process of talent pool planning identifies a group of possible internal replacements for critical positions and also provides developmental opportunities. For our purposes, we will focus on the developmental aspect of the succession planning process.

The components of a successful program identify the qualifications of each leadership position as well as those potential individuals to fill the position. In addition, the program must outline the skills and experiences needed from each potential candidate to prepare that person to fill the position should a vacancy occur. Succession planning and leadership development go hand-in-hand. The succession plan must guide the individual development activities, and the individual development efforts must be tied to the succession plan.

One word of caution: Succession plans will become outdated unless they are regularly updated. Someone must be assigned to monitor the updates. Part of the monitoring and review process involves reviewing talent at least once a year (twice preferred). During this process, each person's development plan should be reviewed and progress evaluated, always making sure the individual's skills and traits are linked to the organization's strategies and goals.

High-Potential Employees

To do succession planning, you must first identify the potential leaders of your organization who will be included in the plan. Once identified, those leaders or high potentials can be targeted for leadership development experiences and assignments. A high-potential employee has the capacity to advance to one of the following: critical position, higher level of responsibility, or higher level of technical proficiency.

Selecting High-Potential Managers

The process for identifying the high potentials includes a combination of approaches, including the following:

- a review and evaluation of current performance because past performance is an indicator of future performance (this means looking for demonstrated desired skills, such as problem-solving ability as well as the ability to learn quickly)
- a thorough assessment of the individual including 360-degree tools, surveys, and interviews (this approach involves the individual as well as others including managers, direct reports, colleagues, mentors, and other leaders)
- observations of on-the-job leadership behaviors (although desired behaviors will vary from organization to organization, high potentials are those who take the initiative, develop new or improve existing processes, volunteer for tough assignments, ask questions, offer solutions, use technology to do things more efficiently, and adapt to change).

Throughout the process of identifying high potentials, keep in mind the competencies that have been identified as a result of the strategic planning process. Once the competencies have been identified, you can develop an individual needs assessment form, such as table 3-1, that leadership development candidates and their managers can use to determine specific competencies that the candidates need to develop. It is a good idea to have candidates complete self-assessments and to have their managers fill out the assessments with specific candidates in mind. Then the managers and candidates meet and compare responses.

Table 3-1. Individual Needs Assessment.

The purpose of this assessment is to help you identify the skill areas you believe you need to further develop to be more effective in your leadership role. The information from the assessment will be compiled to create a group profile that will help determine the focus and content for our leadership development program.

Please rate your skill level (as you perceive it) in each of the following leader competencies.

Key: 5 = Outstanding
4 = Above Average
3 = Average
2 = Below Average
1 = I'm Clueless!

____ **Communicating**

The ability to create an atmosphere of trust and openness that will improve all channels of communication throughout the organization, to communicate skillfully and effectively with people at all levels, and to solicit feedback.

____ **Motivating and Influencing**

The ability to create an environment in which employees feel they are making a real contribution and are eager to come to work and perform at peak capacity and to use reward and recognition techniques to ensure positive, self-directed employee behavior.

____ **Managing and Evaluating Performance**

The ability to set clear, realistic expectations; communicate those expectations; monitor performance; and measure performance on an ongoing basis.

____ **Coaching**

The ability to give ongoing feedback and support to employees to overcome a performance problem or to gain greater competence and to encourage people to do more than they ever imagined they could.

____ **Managing Conflict**

The ability to use proven strategies and techniques to effectively prevent and resolve conflict and to help team members deal with conflict.

___ **Problem Solving and Decision Making**

The ability to use a variety of approaches and techniques to make decisions and solve business problems and to help team members develop those skills as well.

___ **Building an Effective Team**

The ability to work collaboratively with others both inside and outside the department to achieve organizational goals and to create an environment in which team members are interdependent and work together to meet client needs and expectations.

___ **Leading Change**

The ability to lead and manage change within the organization and respond rapidly and effectively to a changing business environment and to help others cope with and manage change.

___ **Planning, Organizing, and Delegating**

The ability to plan and organize work, to determine priorities based on their importance in achieving organizational goals, and to hold oneself and others accountable for reaching those goals.

What management courses, workshops, or seminars have you attended?

What is the most difficult problem or challenge you face in managing people?

Assessing High Potentials

Self-development starts with self-understanding. Self-awareness is key to leadership development and is developed through ongoing feedback. Organizations can help the individual with a candid self-appraisal by providing assessment tools and processes that give the leader or high potential a realistic view of strengths and weaknesses as well as skills gaps. The purpose of an assessment instrument, paper-and-pencil or electronic format, is to provide feedback for self-reflection and examination, identify areas for improvement, or establish a baseline or starting point for future growth. Studies show that the most effective leaders have a strong sense of self-awareness. They understand their character traits, behavioral patterns, value system, and styles of working with others.

The information is gathered from assessment tools, interviews, and even observation on the job or in assessment centers where a person is engaged in structured exercises and given individual feedback on performance by a trained observer. Once the data are collected and analyzed revealing both strengths and developmental needs, the results are shared with the individual, the manager, and the human resource manager. The next step is to develop an individual development plan that identifies specific activities, such as training programs, coaching, job experiences, and other individual and group activities, which are described in detail in chapters 5–7.

Using 360-Degree Feedback

Three hundred sixty–degree feedback (also known as multi-rater feedback) allows an individual to receive behavioral and performance feedback from people at all levels, including those above and below, as well peers, team members, colleagues from other departments, and even customers. It is not a stand-alone event but a process that also includes self-evaluation. The most commonly used assessment for this purpose is the leadership profile. Leadership profiles focus on behaviors the individuals demonstrate that reflect the organization's values and leadership practices. Feedback from a variety of sources helps eliminate bias and provides individuals with valuable information about their behaviors and the consequences of their actions. This information forms the basis for the individual development plans.

Basic Rule 5
People will contribute more if they know where they stand.

Assessment Tools

Types of instruments include surveys, checklists, inventories, questionnaires, and tests. When selecting an assessment instrument, consider the following guidelines:

▶ *Validity*: Does the instrument measure or assess what you want it to measure or assess?

▶ *Reliability*: How accurate is the scoring? Does it yield the same results each time it's administered?

▶ *Theoretical Base*: What is the theory behind the instrument? Does the instrument have a sound theoretical framework?

▶ *Accessibility*: How easy is it to acquire the instrument? Can you purchase it directly from the publisher, or do you have to contact a distributor?

▶ *Fear Factor*: Could the questions, items, or reported results be intimidating? Even those in leadership positions can feel threatened by the assessment process.

▶ *Ease of Scoring*: Is the scoring process easy? How much help will you need to give the participants?

▶ *Ease of Administration*: How complex is the entire process? Do you need to be certified to administer the assessment?

▶ *Interpretation Data*: How meaningful are the interpretations of the data?

▶ *Norms/Comparative Data*: Is comparative data available?

▶ *Time*: How long does it take to complete, score, and discuss the outcomes?

▶ *Cost*: How expensive is the instrument? Is it worth the investment? Can the instrument be used again for other candidates or in training programs, or is it designed for one-time use?

▶ *Copyright*: What are the restrictions for use?

▶ *Facilitator's Guide*: How complete and easy to understand is the facilitator's guide or administration instructions?

Personality Profiles

The following are just a few examples of the many helpful surveys designed to provide insight into an individual's personality and behavior. Keep in mind that in some cases only those with appropriate credentials and certifications can administer the assessment.

Myers-Briggs Type Indicator (MBTI) by Isabel Briggs Myers and Katherine Briggs (Consulting Psychologists Press). A classic in the field, the MBTI is used to understand and appreciate personality differences. Leaders use it to uncover ways to work and interact more effectively with others.

DiSC (Inscape Publishing). The DiSC profile helps people understand themselves and others. This behavioral personality assessment enables people to recognize how they use behavior styles based on their personality and their environment.

LIFO by Stuart Atkins (Business Consultants Network). LIFO identifies each person's orientation to life and work and helps people understand how to work together more effectively.

Leadership Assessments

Numerous leadership assessments are available on the market. First determine what exactly you want to measure and then spend considerable time researching available tools to identify the one that will provide meaningful data for your specific situation. The following are just two examples of leadership assessments.

Leadership Practices Inventory (LPI) by James M. Kouzes and Barry Z. Posner (Pfeiffer). The LPI is a 360-degree leadership assessment tool that helps individuals and organizations measure their leadership competencies.

21st Century Leadership by William Stieber and Karen Lawson (TACTools). This self-assessment gives individuals an opportunity to evaluate their leadership behaviors in six areas or capabilities: Personal Mastery, Future Focused, Innovative Initiative, Organization Development, Organizational Interaction, and Improvement Focused.

Miscellaneous Skills Assessments

Within your leadership development program, you will most likely offer a variety of programs or topics, such as coaching, managing conflict, and managing change. The following are examples of assessments used in both conflict and coaching programs.

Strength Deployment Inventory by Elias Porter (Personal Strengths Publishing). This assessment is designed to give people an opportunity to assess the strengths they use in relating to others under two conditions: when everything is going well and when they are faced with conflict and opposition. This 360-degree process provides insights into the leader's behavior and how others perceive the leader in a work environment. The information helps leaders become more effective in their various work relationships.

Thomas-Kilman Conflict Mode Inventory (TKI) by Kenneth W. Thomas and Ralph H. Kilman (Xicom). TKI is designed to assess an individual's behavior in conflict situations and describes the person's behavior on two dimensions: (1) assertiveness, the extent to which the individual attempts to satisfy his or her concerns and (2) cooperativeness, the extent to which the individual attempts to satisfy the other person's concerns.

Coaching Skills Inventory, 3rd edition, by Kenneth R. Phillips (HRDQ). This instrument is designed to assess the ability of a manager, supervisor, or team leader to recognize when and how to use the skills necessary for conducting effective coaching meetings.

Coaching Power: Performance Improvement and Developmental Inventory by Karen Lawson and William Stieber (TACTools). This tool is for managers or supervisors interested in improving their coaching skills. It provides insight into their own coaching behaviors and introduces them to a structured process to conducting a coaching session. The overall goal is to help individuals enhance their existing coaching skills so that they can help their employees be more effective in their jobs.

The Two Faces of Conflict: Managing Interpersonal and Team Conflict by Karen Lawson and William Stieber (TACTools). This instrument can serve as a useful self-assessment of effective conflict management behaviors. It addresses the phases of conflict management in two situations: (1) interpersonal situations in which the individual is directly involved and (2) team settings where the individual may be helping others resolve conflict. While its purpose is to provide insights into how a person manages conflict, it can also be distributed to others to assess their perception of the respondent's conflict management behaviors.

Assessment/Acceleration Centers

Assessment and acceleration centers help define specific development needs and estimate how far and how fast a candidate will progress. These centers often involve individuals participating in simulations that involve challenges they would face in various leadership positions, such as dealing with employee conflicts, negotiating a merger, handling government officials and inquiries, and responding to the press. The situations require them to make decisions quickly without having all the facts.

Individual Development Plans and Career Development Discussions

The assessment phase results in a leader profile that includes the individual's career track record, results achieved, accomplishments, strengths, development needs, performance ratings, and others' perceptions. After the assessment phase is completed, it's time to map out a development plan. The individual will need help identifying competency gaps as they relate to the organization's short-term and long-term needs as well as its strategic direction.

An individual development plan (IDP) is a formal document that identifies an individual's learning and development goals and how they are to be accomplished. The plan clearly specifies the formal and informal activities and experiences the leader needs to acquire the competencies to meet the IDP goals. The manager and the individual jointly develop the IDP.

To help individuals prepare for the discussion with their managers, ask them to complete the Personal Career Assessment Form in table 3-2.

Table 3-2. Personal Career Assessment Form.

1. How well is your current position suited to your abilities and career objectives for the next 12 months? If not well suited, what would you like to be doing?
2. What are your career goals for the next two to five years?
3. What are you doing (or have you done during the past 12 months) to improve your skills or further your career goals? Include courses, workshops, seminars, and civic and professional activities, emphasizing any leadership skills or development.
4. What specific actions do you plan to take (or would like to take) to achieve your career objectives?

The front-end analysis should have produced developmental plans for each high-potential manager and leader. Each plan should start with development goals established by both the employee and the manager. Based on the desired outcomes, the manager and employee work together to determine the appropriate activities the employee needs to work on to meet the stated goals and satisfy the individual's development needs. These activities will be both individual and group and will involve face-to-face experiences as well as those that are technology based. There must be an integrated approach to the activities, and each activity must have a specific objective. The activities must be chosen purposefully and thoughtfully and be aligned with the organization's strategy as well as with human resource policies and practices. Table 3-3 is an example of an individual development plan. Please note that one of its components is an evaluation section that the individual will complete at the end of the learning experience.

The next step is to select experiences and opportunities that will provide the individual with the tools to move along a career path. With guidance from managers, coaches, and mentors, leaders and potential leaders will choose experiences, such as programs and classes, and opportunities that are linked to their career paths.

Table 3-3. Individual Development Plan.

Employee _____ Department_____

Current Position/Responsibilities_____

Supervisor/Manager_____ Date_____

Directions: Describe below the plan for helping the individual move ahead on a career path. This plan should be developed collaboratively with the employee. Use a separate form for each goal.

Part A: Plan

1. Development Goal: The goal should relate to knowledge, job challenges, or competencies.

   Goal/Need:

2. Development Method: List the methods (training, coaching, mentoring, special assign-ments, etc.) to be used to help the individual meet the goal identified above. For each experience, indicate time schedule and how the individual will apply what is learned.

   Development Method:

   Source/Resource:

   Beginning Date: Expected Date of Completion:

   Application:

   Means of Measurement:

Part B: Progress Checks

1. Progress Check Meetings: The individual and the manager should meet periodically to review progress.

   Date   Outcome

2. Other Monitoring Methods: Identify other methods that were (or will be) used to moni-tor progress.

continued on next page

Table 3-3. Individual Development Plan (continued).

Part C: Development Results

1. Evaluate the learning experience.

   What went well?

   What did you learn?

   How could the experience have been better?

   What challenges or barriers did you encounter in the learning experience?

   What did you do to overcome them?

2. Evaluate the application of the behavior, skill, or knowledge.

   How have you applied the knowledge, skill, behavior, or insights that you gained through the learning experience?

   What challenges have you experienced in trying to apply what you have learned?

   How will you continue to apply what you have learned?

3. Evaluate insights or benefits.

   What additional skills or knowledge did you acquire from your development experience?

   What insights did you gain?

   How will this development experience help you grow as a leader?

Keep in mind that an effective program must have a number of development options tailored to individual needs and aligned with business goals and objectives.

Basic Rule 6
The more voluntary the training, the higher the motivation and involvement of the participants.

Preparation for Development Activities

Once the general discussion about career development has taken place and the development plan is in place (including the selection of development activities with clear linkages to strategic business objectives or goals of the individual), then it is time to prepare the individual for the development experience.

Noted

Research shows that the more supportive and involved managers are the more positive the participants are in the training session.

The effectiveness of training and other learning experiences depends on how well the learner is prepared. The participant's manager is responsible for communicating expectations up front and for reinforcing the skill application on the job. The following guidelines outline the process managers should follow in preparing their direct reports for the development experiences.

Before the Assignment or Experience

Managers of those attending training programs should sit down with their employees and tell them how the training relates to their jobs. Managers should explain what the program is about, tell employees why they are going and what the managers expect the participants to get from the program, and find out what the employees hope to learn. The reality is that this scenario doesn't happen very often. Below are more suggestions for managers before their employees begin the assignment or experience:

▸ Well in advance of the assignment or training session, managers should review performance objectives for the assignment as well as roles and expectations.

▸ For a training program, managers should explain what the program is all about, including objectives and content.

▸ If individuals are attending a program out of town in an unfamiliar setting, managers should explain what they can expect. This should include a discussion of travel arrangements, lodging, and appropriate attire, along with travel-reimbursement policies and procedures.

▶ Managers should tell the individuals what is expected for them to get out of the program or assignment and how it relates to their job or development plan.

▶ Managers should ask individuals what they would like to gain from the program. Encourage them to identify specific skills they would like to develop, information they want to learn, or problems they would like help in solving. Managers should explain that they expect employees to apply what they learn. (This is particularly important for self-study programs because most people who enroll in such programs don't complete them.)

▶ Managers should let individuals know that they will discuss the program or assignment upon completion. Managers might even suggest that the individuals write brief summaries of their learning experience, including what they learned; how they are going to use the training back on the job; and how the training will benefit them, the organization, and, if applicable, their customers. Managers may even want the individuals to share what they learned with their co-workers at a staff meeting.

▶ Employees often worry about being away from the job because of work piling up. Managers should assure them that the work will be there when they get back and not to worry about it. Also, managers should emphasize that they want the individuals to get as much out of the program or assignment as possible.

After the Assignment or Experience

Depending on the length of the assignment or experience, all those involved with the development activity (the individual, manager, trainer, assignment manager, mentor, coach, and so forth) should schedule progress check meetings. The frequency of these meetings will depend on the schedules of the people involved and the complexity of the activities. Once individuals return from the training session, assignment, or other experience, managers must reinforce the learning by discussing outcomes as well as next steps. The following are suggestions for conducting a post-experience debrief with the individuals:

▶ Ask them what they learned and whether it met their expectations.

▶ Center the discussion on how they are going to apply what they learned.

Press them to be specific and ask how you can support them as they try to use what they learned.

▶ Ask them to share their experience, key learning points, and materials with their co-workers.

▶ Follow up over the next few months to make sure they are applying what they learned. After they have had adequate time to use what they learned on the job, ask them what they still want or need to learn.

Think About This

Although you can't make the managers do their jobs in preparing their employees for the training experience, you can prod them a little. Send the managers a memo suggesting how they can help prepare their employees.

Getting It Done

When you conduct multi-session training programs, you can involve the participants' managers in another way. Create homework assignments or projects that the participants must complete outside the sessions, discuss the assignments with their managers, and have the managers sign off. At the end of each session you can also ask the participants to write summaries of what they learned, discuss them with their managers, and be prepared to share the outcomes of their discussion during the next session.

In the next chapter, you will learn how to design and develop a leadership development program.

4

Designing a Leadership Development Program

▪ ▪

What's Inside This Chapter

In this chapter, you'll learn

▶ How to conduct a front-end analysis
▶ The basics of training design
▶ Cooperative learning and active training techniques.

Formal training workshops and seminars are the core of any leadership development program. Although there are standard topics that should be included in all programs, it is important to make sure you are selecting the right modules for the right people and delivering the topics in the appropriate order.

Front-End Analysis

Before you can begin to design and develop a leadership development program, you must conduct a thorough front-end analysis, which serves as the basis for program development and establishes criteria for measuring the success of the program. This will enable you to customize the program to fit the strategies and challenges facing the organization. The process addresses the organizational context including the organization's strategic objectives, major challenges, and the leadership capabilities needed both now and in the future. The design must reflect the organization's leadership competencies. A front-end analysis will help determine the activities necessary to achieve results, but it is essential that you are clear about the desired outcomes before making decisions on what type of training or other activities to provide.

Needs Analysis

The needs analysis process as discussed in this chapter applies primarily to the internal group training program that serves as the core of the organization's comprehensive and integrated leadership development program.

Step One: Identify Organizational Context

To get a clear picture of the leadership development program and its business impact, you should start with senior management. When dealing with senior managers, it is important to ask more strategic questions that address the direction of the organization as well as anticipated industry changes. In other words, you need to start with an organizational context.

Here are some questions that will help you gain a better understanding of the business needs from a more global perspective:

▶ What is the vision of the organization?
▶ What is the mission of the organization?
▶ What are the primary goals and objectives, both short-term and long-term?
▶ What organization or industry issues are driving the need for training?
▶ What is your most critical concern right now?

Of course, learning leaders should already know the answers to these questions; however, some may not depending on their roles and positions in the organization. As a learning leader who will help drive the process, you must know as much as possible about the big picture. If you have not been a part of the strategic planning process, ask to review the strategic plan.

In chapter 3, we discussed the process of assessing leaders and high potentials. Before designing your training program, you must also review the data collected on those individuals. Depending on the size and structure of your organization and the number of leaders and high potentials identified, you may need to create different levels of leadership development training programs such as the following:

- ▶ Level 1: First-line supervisors and those who are likely to be promoted into a supervisory position within a year
- ▶ Level 2: Middle-level managers and assistant managers
- ▶ Level 3: High-level managers, directors, and professionals with no direct reports.

Step Two: Determine Outcomes

Once the need has been determined, you must then define the specific goals the program should meet. The objective must state the desired performance or behavior and be measurable, observable, realistic, and fixable. Working with leaders at various levels, determine what you want to measure and be able to tie it to organizational goals. Do you want to heighten awareness, build skills, change behavior, or modify attitudes and beliefs? You will most likely determine the desired outcomes through your discussions with senior management. These discussions will reveal the gap between the desired and the actual knowledge, skills, and performance of the organization's leaders. The overall goal is to shrink that gap by identifying specific, measurable outcomes and developing programs and initiatives to satisfy the desired outcomes of the leadership development program.

Step Three: Collect Additional Data

In addition to the information you have already collected from senior management and the target audience, you may want to collect more data regarding the target population as a whole rather than as individuals. You may also choose to solicit input from the managers of the target audience. Table 4-1 identifies the advantages and disadvantages of the most common data collection methods.

Questionnaires

A questionnaire is a list of questions used in gathering information on a specific subject. In this case, the subject would be the leader's skills, competencies, qualities, and traits. The questionnaire could be completed by the leader, direct reports, manager, or peers and could be close-ended questions, open-ended questions, or a

Table 4-1. Advantages and Disadvantages of Data-Collection Methods.

Types of Data-Collection Methods	Advantages	Disadvantages
Open-Ended Questionnaires	• Allow respondent to introduce new topics • Easy to develop • Inexpensive to administer	• One-way communication • Intimidating to respondents who may not want to put comments in writing • Prone to ambiguity and opinions
Close-Ended Questionnaires	• Easier to answer • Inexpensive to administer • Ensure feeling of anonymity and confidentiality • Less time consuming	• Limited information • Require more skill and work to prepare • Items subject to misinterpretation • Difficult and time consuming to construct
Instruments	• Validated through research • Quickly and easily administered • Can be administered in groups • Scored quickly	• Need administration and coordination • Difficulty in choosing the most appropriate • Difficult and time consuming to construct • Need to research different types
Interviews	• Can read nonverbal messages • Easier to talk • Build commitment for training • Clarify expectations • Can introduce new topics • More detailed information	• Time consuming • Threatening to some people • Can be affected by interviewer bias • Difficult to organize and analyze data • People may be influenced by peers
Existing Information	• Factual, highly valid information • Easy access to many sources in one place • Inexpensive • Not very time consuming • Unobtrusive • Provide specific examples	• May be outdated • May not cover all areas needed; too generic • May be hard to find or access • Risk misinterpretation • May be biased

combination of both. In a closed-response question, the respondent selects one of two or more answers. An open-response question enables the respondent to write out a short answer.

Instruments

Instruments consist of checklists, inventories, reaction forms, and assessments such as those discussed in chapter 3.

Interviews

One-on-one and group interviews are valuable data sources. When developing your interview questions, be sure to ask open-ended rather than close-ended questions. Close-ended questions can be answered with a simple "yes" or "no." For example, "Do you think there is a need for leadership training?" is designed to elicit a one-word response. You will need to probe further by asking an open-ended question. To get to the heart of the matter right away, ask a question that begins with "how" or "what" such as "What training would help you do your job better or help you develop as a leader?" Try to avoid asking questions that begin with "why." They tend to put people on the defensive.

Plan to take considerable time and care in writing your questions. Not only should they be designed to elicit as much information as possible, but also they must produce answers that will provide meaningful information. Although your questions will vary according to your specific situation, below are some sample questions that may help you in developing your own.

Basic Rule 7
Ask questions that begin with "what" or "how." Avoid questions that begin with "why" because they put people on the defensive.

Target Audience
▶ What is the greatest challenge you face as a manager or leader?
▶ What are the typical situations, customers, or projects that you deal with?
▶ What training have you received to prepare you for this position?
▶ What additional training do you need to help you do your job better?
▶ What do you like best about your job?

▶ How do you know you are doing a good job?

▶ What type of feedback do you receive about your job performance?

▶ How often do you receive feedback?

Managers of Target Audience

▶ What would you like the leaders (or high potentials) who report to you to do differently?

▶ What are the important issues, problems, or changes your direct reports face at the present time?

▶ What skills, knowledge, or behaviors do you think the leaders (or high potentials) in your department need to acquire or improve upon to do their jobs better?

▶ What are the potential barriers that might get in the way of our training efforts?

▶ What methods do you use to measure the performance of the leaders (or high potentials) in your department?

▶ How often do you give feedback to your direct reports about their performance?

▶ What is the biggest challenge you face as a manager?

Existing Information

Existing information may include performance appraisals, exit interviews, turnover records, customer complaints, incident reports, employee grievances, and department audits.

Step Four: Analyze Data

Data analysis can be simple or quite complex, depending on the methods you choose. For qualitative data, such as individual or group interviews, open-ended questionnaires, and observations, you will want to do a content analysis. In a content analysis, you are sorting information into categories (for example, positive and negative reactions) and identifying common themes. The goal of the content analysis is to categorize and quantify the data as much as possible with minimal interpretation.

For quantitative data, such as survey instruments and close-ended questionnaires, you will want to do a statistical analysis. Keep it as simple as possible. Don't allow yourself to become engulfed in number-crunching activities. Look at the data in terms of mean, mode, and median.

During the analysis phase, you are adding to your perceptions of what you think should be addressed in a leadership development training program through qualitative data, such as interviews and focus groups. You will verify your perceptions with survey results and other quantitative data. After you have categorized your data, the next step is to identify priorities, always keeping in mind the business need. Based on your analysis of the data along with your knowledge, experience, and expertise in the field of training and development, you are ready to make your recommendations for specific training programs.

Step Five: Give Feedback

Once the data have been collected and analyzed, you must communicate your conclusions and recommendations to key personnel. This feedback should be delivered in both a written and an oral format. You need to plan a strategy for presenting the information in a positive light. As you prepare to communicate your findings and recommendations, think through what (and how much) to share, how to share, and with whom to share your findings and recommendations.

Written Report

The final report is a critical piece. It should be constructed in such a way that it presents the data in an easy-to-understand format along with conclusions and recommendations. The length of the final report, of course, depends on the extensiveness of your assessment. In any case, the written report should contain the following elements:

▶ *Executive Summary.* You should provide an executive summary that provides an overview of your proposal. This summary is an abbreviated, concise representation of your document, limited to one page and distributed to key stakeholders.

▶ *Description of the Process.* This section provides the appropriate background information and briefly describes the entire needs assessment process, including purpose, scope, methods used, and people involved. Be sure to include your rationale.

▶ *Summary of Findings.* In this section, present your data clearly and concisely, highlighting patterns or significant results.

▶ *Preliminary Conclusions.* This section addresses your analysis of the data, focusing on the key issues that have surfaced. It may be appropriate to show

how the findings relate to or support your (or others') perceptions or intuition. Point out how the issues relate to the business need.

▶ *Potential Barriers.* Take a proactive approach by addressing potential barriers up front and suggesting ways to overcome them. Potential barriers can be almost anything, but the most common will probably be cost, time commitment, and the commitment of the target audience as well as their managers.

Oral Presentation

In addition to the written proposal, you should plan on presenting your information and recommendations to a selected audience. The oral presentation gives you an opportunity to get reactions from the key players. Be prepared for questions and challenges. Anticipate what they may be, and have your responses ready. Look at your presentation as a chance to sell your ideas and reaffirm senior-level commitment to and support for the leadership development process. That means you will need to fine-tune your persuasion and influencing skills.

Commitment from the Top

A successful leadership development program starts at the top. Senior line managers must own leadership development. Strong support by the CEO and other executives is essential and includes not only financial support but also active participation. By involving line management and other key players in your organization from the beginning, you will get the support you need for the program to succeed. Because they have had input, they will have a vested interest in the program. You will gain management commitment if managers and supervisors see that you are developing training programs in direct response to their specific needs. Once you have received approval, you are now ready to design the training program.

Members of executive leadership need to participate as learners and also as faculty as we will discuss in more detail in chapter 5. Further credibility is established when executives serve as guest instructors or lecturers. Furthermore, it gives those at the top the opportunity to share their visions and, at the same time, learn from the participants. It also establishes a common language of leadership for the organization.

The CEO and the direct reports should be the first to go through the program. In fact, they should be designated the pilot group so they can, if necessary, suggest modifications to the program to ensure it is in sync with the organization's vision, values, and strategies. Another reason for their participation is so they can reinforce,

> ## Think About This
>
> Begin to develop a list of leaders in the organization you would like to invite to participate as faculty. Consider their skills, personalities, areas of responsibilities, and roles in helping to sell the program. Then meet with them one-on-one to solicit their input, support, and participation as instructors.

support, and coach those who report to them as they go through the program and apply what they learned to those who report to them. Finally, top management's participation sends a clear message throughout the organization that this program is important.

For a leadership development program to be successful, senior line managers must be held accountable for the ongoing development of the leadership talent in their business units. In fact, their bonus compensation should be tied to their efforts to develop people. Another way to communicate and demonstrate commitment is to create an advisory board composed of the senior people who head business units. Their job is to make sure that the program stays on track. Their responsibilities include oversight in terms of quality of program content and delivery, alignment with strategic objectives, and the selection of high-potential managers to participate in the program.

Program Design

Once you have completed the front-end analysis, communicated your findings, and received top management support, you are ready to design the core program.

Approaches

The approaches and methods are as varied as the participants themselves. The specific topics are determined by both the individual's and organization's needs as identified in the front-end analysis and are always tied to the strategic plan. The specifics will be addressed in chapters 5–7. It's important to use a variety of learning methods and to choose methods that achieve learning objectives. Regardless of the specific methods (lecture, case studies, group discussion, and so forth), your design and selection should be based on the principles and practices of active training.

Based on what we know about adult learning, learning styles, and the characteristics of learners, active training is the most effective means of delivering classroom training. Research shows that people understand concepts better and retain information longer when they are actively involved in the learning process.

Basic Rule 8
People learn by doing, not by being told.

The active-training approach, however, requires the trainer to think through the design thoroughly. The trainer must spend time visualizing how the activity will play out, dealing with logistics, anticipating participants' reactions, and identifying potential problems. Active training is based on a well-researched, proven approach to learning called cooperative learning.

Cooperative Learning

Cooperative learning is based on two assumptions: (1) learning by nature is an active endeavor, and (2) different people learn in different ways.

Cooperative learning is not simply putting people in pairs or groups and asking them to work on an assignment. The approach must be carefully planned and orchestrated by a skilled facilitator who composes and arranges learning experiences. Participants work in concert, encouraging and facilitating each other's efforts to achieve, complete tasks, and reach the group's goals. For this to happen, the trainer must function as an observer, adviser, coach, and consultant throughout the cooperative learning activity.

Noted

Studies over the past 125 years show that cooperative learning produced higher achievement, more positive relationships among participants, and healthier adjustment than individualistic experiences.

Active Learning

In an active learning environment, the instructional design should maximize the effectiveness of instruction for both the learner and the trainer.

We know that a safe, positive environment is critical to a successful learning experience. The creation of such an environment begins with the physical setting. By using music, posters, and props, the instructor creates a mood and sets the tone for the learning experience. Beginning the class with an icebreaker, opener, or other active-learning technique will help learners focus on the course content and get them involved immediately. Other set-induction techniques such as showing a film clip or displaying a photo, artifact, or cartoon and asking participants to comment is an excellent way to build interest and prepare the participants for the learning that follows.

An integral part of the physical environment involves the actual seating arrangements. Recognizing that instructors are often faced with room sizes and configurations that are less than ideal, it is important to determine the type of interaction you desire, then arrange the seating to achieve the desired results. For example, the U-shape configuration is very effective in promoting group interaction with a minimum of trainer control.

Another way in which trainers can create a positive learning environment is to find out what participants think and feel about the subject well in advance so that this information can be used to design active-learning activities that take into account individual differences and levels of experience. This can be accomplished through pre-session surveys and phone calls to participants. On-the-spot assessment through opening activities can also help the trainer learn about participants' knowledge, attitudes, and experience.

Strategies and Techniques

The following strategies and techniques characterize the successful implementation of cooperative learning in an adult training environment.

Structure and Organization. Cooperative learning is characterized by structured learning groups. The trainer places participants in specific groups and gives specific assignments with clear instructions and time limits. These assignments may include group tasks as well as individual roles, such as recorder, timekeeper, or spokesperson.

Moderate Level of Content. Because cooperative-learning programs focus more on process than content, program designers should be guided in their design by determining need to know versus nice to know. Content is no longer limited to facts, dates, formulas, and definitions. It has been redefined to include skills and understanding, thus ensuring a balance among the cognitive, affective, and behavioral domains of learning. By clearly defining what you want participants to know and be able to do by the end of the class, you will clarify content and select appropriate learning strategies.

High Level of Participation. The trainer's role is that of a facilitator whose primary function is to manage the learning process. Learners are actively engaged in activities from the start, continually involved in doing, discussing, and reflecting.

Interdependence. One of the primary purposes of cooperative learning is to create interdependence among group members. To facilitate that outcome, the trainer requires all group members to master the content of the assignment and then teach content to each other.

Minimal Lecture. Although lecture has its place as a training method, it should be used in small doses of 10 to 15 minutes. Based on research conducted during the 1960s, lengthy, uninterrupted periods of teacher-centered discourse result in confusion, boredom, and low retention. Lectures, however, need not relegate learners to a passive role. Learners can be involved through various interactive techniques that promote both understanding and retention.

Variety of Methods. "Small groups" is a term that may be used for groups of five to seven as well as for pairs and trios. In any case, small groups are effective. They not only incorporate all the elements of active learning, but also help develop interpersonal skills and provide those who might be reticent to participate in a risk-free environment in which to express opinions or ask questions.

Peer Teaching. We know from our study of adult learning theory that adults bring a wealth of experience and expertise to the learning environment. Encouraging them to draw on and share their experiences with others in the group can be rewarding for both the trainer and the participants.

Iterative Process. Throughout the session, the trainer arranges activities that build on and somewhat repeat concepts and skills learned earlier. In this manner, learning material is reinforced and participants have more opportunities to digest and integrate the material into their current body of knowledge and understanding.

Real-World Application. Through many of the methods described above, participants are able to use real-life situations in learning new concepts and skills. Sometimes the trainer solicits examples of hypothetical or real problems for the participants to use throughout the session. In addition, before the session ends, the trainer gives participants the opportunity to develop individual action plans, identifying how they are going to apply what they have learned in the real world.

Resources for Activities and Materials

Once you have decided upon the content and have some idea of the methods and materials you want to use to get the content across to your participants, the next step is to come up with specific activities or structured experiences and specific training aids. As you are developing your leadership development training program, you will need to make the decision to use materials and activities already developed or to create your own.

Although you will, of course, want to develop your own active-training activities, you will still need to go to other sources for methods and materials such as videos and assessment instruments. You will also find that in some situations you must lecture. All of these tried-and-true instructional methods, even lecture, can be redesigned to involve the participants more actively.

Many trainers, particularly those new to the field and often those faced with time and cost constraints, choose to use off-the-shelf training materials that they integrate into their own designs. Most good trainers use a combination of developing their own, buying, customizing, and tailoring.

Before you jump headlong into the process of investigating resources for your activities and materials or develop your own, you need to consider several key factors that will influence your decision.

Time

Course or program development takes time—a lot of time. Coming up with your own activities, exercises, assessment instruments, role plays, and case studies can take hours, days, or even weeks. Many people are surprised to discover, however, that the process of locating the most appropriate activity or even video for a given situation is also extremely time consuming.

Cost

Cost plays an important role also. If you develop your own materials, you must take into consideration your salary per hour as well as the salaries of any support personnel involved. Even if you spend time selecting published material, you must also factor in the cost of your research time. Then, of course, if you do use published materials, you will have costs associated with purchasing or licensing—costs you will incur each time you deliver the program.

Quality

The quality of the materials and activities is also important. Quality can relate to the actual appearance of the materials, the credibility of the content, or the level of detail provided.

Suitability

Your biggest concern should be the appropriateness of the activity or material for your purposes. You must take into consideration the audience, the topic, and your objective. Does each proposed activity or material do what you want it to do?

Experience and Expertise

You must also evaluate your own skills and abilities. If you want to develop your own role play or case study, you need to consider your level of creativity as well as your writing ability. In other words, only you can determine your comfort level, skill, and experience in developing your own activities and materials.

Skill Application

By its very nature, an active training approach to program design provides many opportunities for participants to practice the skills they learned and to receive feedback on how well they demonstrated those skills. To help them succeed, the trainer will need to coach them as they practice the skills in the training session. In addition, they will want and need to apply the skills in the workplace. This can be accomplished by giving them specific assignments at the end of each session in a multi-session program as discussed in chapter 3.

Developing leaders is a long-term effort—there is no quick fix. An effective leadership development program must be designed as an ongoing process, not a series of events, and should involve more frequent, ongoing learning experiences.

A successful, integrated leadership development program employs and incorporates a variety of individual and group activities that will be described in more detail in chapters 5–7.

 ### Getting It Done

Begin designing your leadership development core program by listing the topics you are going to address. Then research the topics to determine content. Once you have identified content points, think about the methods you are going to use to communicate the content.

For more detailed information on how to design and develop an active-training program, refer to *The Trainer's Handbook* by Karen Lawson (2006).

In the next chapter, you will learn about incorporating formal internal group programs into the overall leadership development program.

5

Formal Internal Group Programs

What's Inside This Chapter

In this chapter, you'll learn

▶ About corporate universities
▶ How to select external consultants
▶ About action learning
▶ Group mentoring strategies
▶ The use of business simulations.

Formal internal group programs involve selected leaders and high potentials who will participate in group activities and programs designed or developed by internal staff. These programs may include seminars, group projects, mentoring programs, and business simulations. Many of the leadership development programs and initiatives delivered by organizations are offered through an increasingly popular concept—the corporate university.

Corporate Universities

Corporate universities (CUs) are no longer just for large organizations such as McDonald's, Motorola, General Electric, and Disney. Even small and medium-sized companies are adopting or adapting the concept and practice of the university model. The term *university*, however, is a misnomer because a true university is an educational institution that grants degrees. CUs, however, offer company-specific and often job-specific training to their employees. The corporate university approach tends to be more structured, organized, and integrated into the organization's overall strategic plan. Because the corporate university model continues to grow in popularity, this chapter will address its role in developing current and future leaders in an organization.

Much like a traditional university (and sometimes partnering with), a CU offers both traditional in-person and online courses. CUs are generally organized into colleges, such as the leadership college, sales college, operational effectiveness college, business skills college, and customer service college. Because of their formalized structure, CUs are able to develop a standardized and comprehensive leadership development curriculum. Furthermore, senior management is more involved with the learning process, frequently serving as faculty and thus facilitating more interaction with high potentials. Senior leaders are involved, identifying the company's primary challenges and determining what knowledge and competencies leaders need to outperform the competition.

One of the premier examples of the "leaders as teachers" concept was implemented at Becton, Dickinson, & Co., a global medical technology company, in 2000 by then–vice president of talent management and chief learning officer Edward Betof. According to Betof in an interview, who is currently senior fellow and academic director of the executive program in work-based learning leadership at the University of Pennsylvania (the first-of-its-kind program for chief learning officers and other learning leaders), a corporate university's "success depends on alignment with the company's business strategy, purpose, and values. A chief learning officer must listen hard as to what the company is and where it's going."

As a result of the direct involvement of the organization's leaders as teachers, the course offerings and content are more directly related to the current and future leadership needs of the organization. In a "leaders as teachers" program, there is a mutual learning experience for both teachers and learners. Participants benefit from interacting with leaders on a more personal level, and teachers get to know employees better and gain greater insight into people's leadership potential. Furthermore, teachers develop their teaching, facilitating, coaching, and mentoring skills far beyond what their normal day-to-day responsibilities require. When they prepare to teach, they gain additional knowledge about various areas of the business, and they come in contact with other leaders in a different context and venue. To ensure the quality of instruction, all internal faculty must participate in a train-the-trainer program. They should also be evaluated on an ongoing basis.

Noted

The leaders who teach often gain as much or more from the experience than the learners.

CUs are usually more cost effective than external leadership development programs. CUs take longer and are most costly to establish, but the long-term benefits are worth it. Because everything is done in-house, including using employees as faculty members, designing and developing the programs, and using internal meeting facilities, the company will save money. Other intangible benefits include developing a sense of community, creating informal mentoring relationships, and building powerful personal and professional networks.

Seminars and Guest Speakers

The basic format for leadership development training in most organizations has been and will continue to be a series of in-house seminars delivered by an internal training person or an outside consulting firm. The decision of which to use is determined by a number of factors, such as the expertise and availability of the organization's training staff as well as cost and time constraints. Regardless of who designs and delivers the program, one thing is certain: The program must reflect the organization's management philosophy and desired leadership competencies and practices. Although the specific modules will be driven by the needs assessment process we discussed in chapter 4, core leadership competencies are addressed through the following topics.

Keep in mind that the outline is merely an example of what you may want to include in your program. You will determine the topics for your specific program based on the findings from your needs assessment.

Understanding Leadership
▶ Definition of leadership
▶ Qualities and characteristics of effective leaders
▶ Styles of leadership

Communicating and Influencing
▶ Listening actively
▶ Communicating nonverbally
▶ Delivering your message
▶ Adapting your style
▶ Using email effectively

Motivating and Retaining Employees
▶ Understanding today's employees
▶ Managing across generations
▶ Creating the environment

Leading Change
▶ Nature of change
▶ Reactions to change
▶ Strategies for managing change
▶ Overcoming resistance to change

Dealing with Conflict
▶ Recognizing symptoms and causes of conflict
▶ Preventing conflict
▶ Dealing with conflicting values
▶ Resolving conflict

Delegating
▶ Opportunities to delegate
▶ Delegation of authority with responsibility
▶ Delegation process

Coaching
- ▶ Coaching versus counseling
- ▶ Barriers to coaching
- ▶ Coaching process
- ▶ Characteristics of effective coaches
- ▶ Coaching pitfalls

Managing Performance
- ▶ Setting clear standards and expectations
- ▶ Giving feedback
- ▶ Holding people accountable
- ▶ Managing from a distance
- ▶ Evaluating performance

Conducting Effective Meetings
- ▶ Running meetings on time and target
- ▶ Understanding group processes
- ▶ Holding teleconferences and videoconferences

Developing Employees
- ▶ Onboarding/Orienting new employees
- ▶ Mentoring
- ▶ Training
- ▶ Career planning

Managing Priorities and Stress
- ▶ Managing your minutes and yourself
- ▶ Recognizing causes and symptoms of stress
- ▶ Helping others manage stress
- ▶ Maintaining work-life balance.

The length and frequency of the sessions will depend on the program's overall requirements and specifications. Ideally, each of these modules should be a full-day session delivered in an active-training format that would have the most effect. The reality of life is that others will often dictate how much time is available to design and deliver the training program. Those who do not understand the difference between (and benefits of) an active, experiential approach to training and lecture-driven, instructor-centered training may expect you to cover the material in two-hour segments. This is where it is extremely important for you as a learning leader to identify your objectives and desired outcomes quite clearly. Be realistic about what you can and cannot accomplish within the prescribed timeframe. If the organization is committed to leadership skill development and behavior change, then adequate time must be allotted for that to happen.

External Consultants

As more organizations downsize their human resource or training departments, they look to outside service providers. This belt tightening also results in more service providers competing for business in the marketplace. With so many resources available, how does the client choose the right consultant for the right project? In many cases, the person assigned to select an external consultant may not know where to begin the search.

The following sources can help save time and money in identifying potential outside resources:

▶ internal sources (managers or other human resource professionals)
▶ colleagues in other organizations
▶ professional organizations
▶ consultants that the organization has used before
▶ industry publications.

Once you have identified and narrowed the list of potential training consultants, the next challenge is to choose the one with the best fit for your particular organization and project. Use the following checklist to help make the right choice:

▶ experience in your industry
▶ knowledge and experience with the topic
▶ length of time in business
▶ knowledge of your industry
▶ knowledge of your organization
▶ knowledge and experience in the field of human resource development
▶ track record of results
▶ quality of materials
▶ image/professionalism

- ▶ involvement in professional organizations
- ▶ representative clients
- ▶ publications
- ▶ geographic locations
- ▶ available resources
- ▶ approach/philosophy
- ▶ fees
- ▶ ability to identify need
- ▶ degree of flexibility
- ▶ level of commitment.

Begin to evaluate consultant candidates by carefully reviewing the consultants' written materials, keeping in mind these materials have been designed and written as selling tools.

When you interview potential service providers, use behavioral interviewing skills and open-ended questions to identify whether the consultant meets a particular criterion. For example, if you want to know about the consultant's track record, you might ask, "Tell me about your most successful client experience." Other probing questions might include the following:

- ▶ What do you think is the most important aspect of a client-consultant relationship?
- ▶ What do you know about our organization?
- ▶ What sets you apart from other consultants?
- ▶ How long have you been in business?
- ▶ What has been the most challenging consulting project you have ever had?
- ▶ How large is your organization?

Because training is a process, not a series of events, it is important to incorporate real-world application opportunities into the program. To ensure transfer of learning from the classroom to the workplace, participants should develop individual action plans at the end of each session and be held accountable for implementing those plans back on the job. In addition, they should be given assignments between sessions. These assignments should be related directly to the session topic and should reflect practical application of the skills and strategies addressed in each session.

Action Learning

Action learning is a real-time learning experience that occurs on the job and with the dual—and equally important—purposes in mind of (1) addressing a business need and (2) developing individuals by exposing them to important, challenging, and useful learning experiences. Action learning is especially useful when the talents of many organizational functions, groups, or processes should be brought together. It responds to management needs by encouraging colleagues to meet together in groups for the purpose of solving organizational problems.

In action learning, the problem or project becomes the central learning experience. Participants are encouraged to learn from their attempts to solve a problem and then reflect on their decisions and behaviors during the process. Action learning groups generally consist of four to eight members from diverse backgrounds or areas of the organization. Group meetings (outside the classroom environment) serve as a source of pressure on members to keep working on the project.

Action Learning Projects

Participants will be involved in an action learning process that will incorporate and enable them to develop and apply the following leadership skills: teamwork, problem solving, communication, goal setting, influencing, and coaching. Each person will have an opportunity to participate in both a facilitation and presentation skill practice.

Important elements of action learning are the learning group, the obligation to implement solutions to real problems, individual and group accountability, and experiential learning.

The goal of the action learning process is to encourage employee development while solving or attempting to solve real-life problems. Action learning demonstrates the power of learning while doing. The project is the learning based on real-life leadership projects within the organization. It focuses on complex problems that touch a number of parts of the organization. Action learning also compels the participants to become aware of their own values and beliefs; it demands that they be aligned with present realities. It combines self-awareness and leadership skills that are required to move the organization forward. Furthermore, action learning provides an opportunity for senior organizational leaders to coach program participants.

In action learning, team members research the topic, present the plan, and execute it. Projects can last a few weeks or a year, depending on the nature of the project.

The following is a list of potential projects for a range of action learning groups:

- ▶ increasing productivity
- ▶ succession planning
- ▶ improving various processes or systems
- ▶ developing benchmarks for performance
- ▶ strategic planning
- ▶ developing a customer profitability system
- ▶ increasing sales
- ▶ improving corporate communication
- ▶ designing a mentoring program
- ▶ developing a wellness program
- ▶ designing an employee reward and recognition program.

Benefits of Action Learning

Action learning is a very effective leadership development technique. Because it is an active learning process, individuals learn more rapidly and are able to apply their knowledge and skills immediately. Those who participate in action learning projects benefit in the following ways:

- ▶ They develop critical thinking skills along with questioning and problem-solving skills.
- ▶ They learn how to be effective team members.
- ▶ They gain more knowledge about the organization's people, products, and processes.
- ▶ They develop presentation and facilitation skills.
- ▶ They improve communication skills, including giving and receiving feedback.
- ▶ They develop networks and relationships with others in the organization.
- ▶ They gain fresh perspectives.
- ▶ They learn new problem-solving approaches.

Basic Rule 9

People are motivated to learn when they see relevance to their real-life situations and are able to apply what they learned as quickly as possible.

Group Mentoring

Mentoring is a process that focuses on providing guidance, direction, and career advice. Group mentoring involves senior leaders who take the initiative to share their knowledge with the group that consists of four to six high-performing protégés. They serve as leaders of group learning and facilitators of group growth. The group itself is responsible for setting the agenda with the group mentor serving as a resource. Members of the group should be chosen with care and should represent a diversity of position levels, functions, race, gender, and career goals (Kaye and Scheef, 2000). The protégé group meets with the mentor each month for several hours during which the group explores issues or concerns they have identified. The group mentor should encourage members of the group to think critically and strategically by looking at various options and challenging their traditional beliefs. The word *think* is critical. It is the mentor's job to push back and make the protégés really think about the issues. The mentor facilitates the process in which the protégés arrive at their own answers or solutions to the problems they are presented.

As a resource person, the mentor may suggest articles or books for the group members to read and then discuss at a meeting. The mentor can also be helpful by sharing experiences as they relate to the topic and encourage the protégés to share their experiences as well.

Think About This

To help build support for mentoring in your organization, interview leaders at various levels and ask them about their experiences with mentoring from the perspective of a protégé. Have they had mentors? How did the mentors help them develop in their careers? Collect the responses and use them in internal marketing efforts and also as part of the mentor and protégé training.

Learning Teams

Learning teams are groups of individuals who meet on a regular basis (such as monthly) to focus on a particular area of common interest. The purpose is to support individual growth and learning. These groups tend to be informal and meet at times when people are more likely to attend, such as lunchtime or early morning.

There may be a designated facilitator chosen from the group, or the group may elect to rotate facilitation responsibilities. This format may be particularly helpful for emerging leaders who want to address issues and challenges they face in supervising others, learning about new technology, developing a skill such as public speaking, or sharing best practices. Often they invite guest speakers from both inside and outside the organization to enhance their knowledge and skills when no formal training is available in a particular subject area. You may want to come up with interesting and attention-getting program titles such as "Business and Bagels" or "Lunch and Learn."

Business Simulations

For our purposes, the term *simulation* refers to lengthy, case-like scenarios that simulate problems in the work environment. The design is complicated, often requiring participants to make decisions at various points throughout the activity. The most well-known simulations are the consensus-seeking survival simulations used in sessions dealing with teamwork.

Participants can't just be plopped into a simulation experience. For simulations to be successful, they must have the following components (Billhardt, 2008):

1. The organization must have clearly defined leadership competencies stated in behavioral terms. These competencies must reflect the organization's culture, mission, vision, and strategy.
2. Participants need to be prepared for the simulation experience. Prior to engaging in the activity, leaders need to go through a process of self-awareness and insight into their strengths and weaknesses. In other words, they need to have a clear understanding of the desired competencies they need to improve. This can be accomplished through the use of self-assessment tools and feedback.
3. The simulations need to be carefully designed and engineered to give all the participants an opportunity to experience challenging real-world situations where they can practice new behavior without the consequences of real-world failure.
4. The experience needs to be reinforced with appropriate feedback and follow-up. Participants should leave the simulation with specific action plans that include coaching, mentoring, and other learning activities that

61

will span a designated period of months or weeks following the simulation activity.

Below are two types of simulations that can be beneficial to leaders.

Paper-and-Pencil Simulations

Business simulations also fall into this category. Generally, business simulations are tied to management or financial disciplines and address a specific skill within that discipline, such as problem solving, delegation, coaching and counseling, or planning. Unlike the survival simulations, the business game presents realistic management situations that test participants' knowledge and skill.

Survival simulations and business simulations are generally lengthy, requiring anywhere from one to three hours to complete and process. They are a great way to sharpen analytical thinking, tasks, and people skills, and simulations help participants gain insight into their own behavior as they interact with others.

Computer-Based Simulations

More and more organizations are using computer simulations as part of their training programs. Computer-based leadership simulations are designed to replicate real-world situations a leader might experience, such as making decisions, dealing with conflict, handling personnel problems, and managing multiple priorities. The use of simulations (ranging from several hours to several days) is more successful in changing behavior and developing competencies than traditional learning methods because participants are practicing their leadership skills in difficult real-world situations and receiving immediate feedback from the facilitators and their peers.

Distance Learning and Coaching

Distance learning implies a virtual classroom in which the instructor and participants interact via video or audio connections from one or more locations. More and more organizations are supplementing or even converting their classroom-based courses to distance learning venues. In leadership development training, distance learning is not as effective as face-to-face interaction because many of the nonverbal cues and other nuances are lost. This lack of direct contact can be compensated for by having a trained facilitator present in each of the participant locations. The on-site facilitators will be responsible for promoting discussion among the participants at that location and engaging them in group activities initiated by the off-site lead facilitator. If distance learning is used, bring all the participants together for one or two days of face-to-face interaction before using the video or audio technology. That enables people to get to know each other, which will, in turn, enhance the learning process.

On-site facilitators will conduct coaching between training sessions. The purpose of these sessions is for the participants to discuss challenges they experience as they apply what they learned in the previous class sessions. The length and frequency of the sessions will vary depending on the group's needs and desired outcomes.

Getting It Done

Make a list of all the formal internal group training and development experiences that could apply to your organization. Then develop a plan with a timeline as to when you are going to implement them. Be realistic about the amount of time it will take.

In the next chapter, you will learn about the individual development activities you can incorporate into your leadership development program.

6

Individual Development Activities

■ ■

What's Inside This Chapter

In this chapter, you'll learn

▶ About executive coaching
▶ The elements of a mentoring program
▶ How to use special assignments as part of leadership development
▶ How networking can enhance leadership development
▶ How to use distance learning as a development activity.

In addition to (or in place of) group learning experiences, the organization should develop a cadre of individual development activities. These activities must be incorporated into the overall leadership development and also must be tailored to each individual and the person's specific development needs. A number of activities are available, ranging from simple to complex, short-term to long-term, and low-cost to expensive.

Executive Coaching

One of the most popular and effective individual activities is executive coaching. Executive coaching is a one-on-one collaborative process to help executives and managers improve or enhance their management or interpersonal skills by gaining greater competence and confidence and overcome barriers to improving performance. Coaching builds on the person's strengths and reframes negative situations so that the individual can eliminate self-limiting thinking and behaviors and become the high-potential, high-performing person that is desired.

What Does the Coach Do?

A coach is not a psychotherapist, counselor, mentor, or consultant. The coach challenges, listens, remains objective, offers support and encouragement, and maintains confidentiality. A coach helps people do the following:

- ▶ focus on the present and future
- ▶ define goals, dreams, passion, and vision
- ▶ identify strengths and opportunities for learning and growth
- ▶ set concrete, measurable goals
- ▶ create and execute an action plan that gets desired results.

A coach leads the person through a process of self-discovery and self-directed problem solving. Furthermore, the coach pushes the person to stretch and to achieve and holds the individual accountable. Coaches conduct sessions face-to-face or on the telephone at times that are mutually convenient.

Types of Coaching

There are two major categories of executive coaching: content coaching and development coaching.

Content Coaching

Content coaching provides the person with the knowledge and skills in a specific content area and is conducted by an expert in that area. For example, if an individual needs to improve presentation skills, an expert is brought in to work with the leader one-on-one. In other cases, the leader may need to know more about some area of the business in a specific industry. An example of this would be a physician who needs to know how to run a practice as a business. Another example is an attorney who needs help with business development. The basis of the coaching process is the development of a learning plan with specific timelines and activities to achieve specific outcomes. Activities include reading assignments followed by debriefing with the coach, role plays, and application assignments between coaching sessions.

Development Coaching

Development coaching helps the leader develop and fine-tune the skills, knowledge, and attitudes to support the organization's leadership values and philosophies. The overall goal of development coaching is for the individual to become more effective in relating to and interacting with others. The process involves identifying behaviors that negatively affect the individual's interactions with others, developing an action plan, and coaching the candidate to change limiting behaviors. The following is a brief overview of the development coaching process.

Information Gathering. The coach meets with the candidate's manager to gain insight into the circumstances and issues that have precipitated the request for individual coaching. The discussion will also focus on the context and environment in which the candidate operates as well as the individuals with whom the individual interacts.

Meeting with the Candidate. The coach meets with the coaching candidate and gives an overview of the process and discusses the circumstances that have created the need for the coaching. During this session, they discuss the candidate's awareness of the situation and commitment to changing behavior. The coach will also ask the candidate to complete a questionnaire providing some basic background information.

Interviewing Key People. The coach meets with key designated individuals within the organization who can provide information on the following:

- ▶ history of the candidate
- ▶ effective accomplishments
- ▶ ineffective practices

- ▸ understanding of current responsibilities
- ▸ why this person is valued
- ▸ specific outcomes they want from the coaching process
- ▸ culture of the organization
- ▸ values of the organization.

Assessing the Candidate. Based on the information from the interviews, candidate's questionnaire, and meetings with the candidate and the manager, the coach selects the appropriate assessment instrument(s) to help the candidate in the change efforts. The candidate completes a self-assessment, and a feedback version of the instrument is distributed to the appropriate people for their input. All assessments are completed and sent directly to the coach to ensure anonymity and confidentiality.

Analyzing Data. The coach reviews all the information from the candidate and others. This review enables the coach to identify patterns of behavior that are positive and those that need to change. The coach then prepares to share the results with the candidate, candidate's manager, and director of human resources.

Developing an Action Plan. The coach meets with the candidate's manager and director of human resources to share results from the analysis phase. The coach then meets with the candidate to share the results of the assessments and gives feedback about behavior strengths and those that need to change. The candidate is encouraged to share reaction to the feedback. The coach and the candidate work together to develop an action plan for improvement and to establish a schedule for the coaching sessions. Following the meeting with the candidate, the coach meets again with the candidate's manager and director of human resources to discuss outcomes resulting from the session with the candidate.

Coaching. Each coaching session lasts an average of 60 to 90 minutes. These sessions can take place via telephone or face-to-face meetings. Together, the coach and candidate work on the action plan and chart progress on the behavior changes.

Mentoring

Mentoring is becoming an increasingly important component of leadership development as a means of increasing political savvy, exposure, and visibility within the organization. As is the case with group mentoring discussed in chapter 5, one-on-one mentoring can be conducted face-to-face or via telephone, email, video conferencing (or a combination of venues). The old patriarchal approach to mentoring has been replaced by a more collaborative relationship in which the mentor and protégé work together as partners to achieve the protégé's development goals.

Mentoring programs may be formal (with corporate sponsorship) or informal (spontaneous with few guidelines). In fact, in the past, mentors typically picked their protégés, taking them under their wings as the heir apparent to succeed the mentor in the leadership position. The trend today is toward a more structured approach in which mentors and protégés are matched and the mentoring process is prescribed by the organization. This more formalized approach is more effective in developing future leaders.

What Is a Mentor?

A mentor acts as a trusted adviser, coach, teacher, role model, and sponsor who establishes and maintains a relationship with a less-experienced person. The mentor may also act as a referral agent or advocate for the protégé within a company. The mentor assists the protégé with the transition into the company structure and with learning the finer points of the institutional culture. A mentor provides the support and expertise needed for continued professional growth.

What Does a Mentor Do?

More specifically, the mentor fulfills the following roles and functions:

- acts as a positive role model who leads by example
- assists the protégé in understanding organizational culture, policy, and procedure
- provides support and company information to the protégé for the purpose of furthering the protégé's growth and development
- assists the protégé with establishing short- and long-term career goals
- provides reinforcement and informal assessment of work
- provides strategies for overcoming obstacles
- expands the protégé's professional network and resources inside and outside the organization
- imparts knowledge regarding career progression

- ▶ acts as the protégé's advocate within the company
- ▶ motivates the protégé to take the initiative in work and in professional development
- ▶ assists the protégé with problem solving related to career and work issues
- ▶ gives inside information on the way the company works
- ▶ builds the protégé's confidence
- ▶ gives constructive feedback.

The Selection Process

Participation in a mentoring program should be voluntary. The mentor should not be the protégé's supervisor. It's important that both parties communicate candidly. The relationship also requires mutual trust, openness, and accountability. As part of the structured process, the organization needs to adopt and adhere to a set of specific selection criteria. At a minimum, mentors should have the following qualities and characteristics:

- ▶ have strong interpersonal and communication skills
- ▶ value the company
- ▶ be positive role models
- ▶ be able to coach and give feedback
- ▶ be sensitive to the protégé's needs
- ▶ care about helping and developing others
- ▶ understand the dynamics of the organization
- ▶ be open and willing to share experiences
- ▶ be accessible.

By the same token, protégés must possess certain skills and characteristics:

- ▶ desire to learn
- ▶ willingness to accept feedback
- ▶ ability to be introspective
- ▶ openness to new ideas
- ▶ commitment to career growth and development.

Of course, the organization may add other desired skills and characteristics that are linked to the desired leadership competencies and the company's strategic direction. The important thing is that everyone needs to clearly understand the reasons for and expectations of the mentoring program.

Mentor and Protégé Training

Mentors and protégés will need training on what a mentoring process is and how to make the relationship work. Training should include the following topics:

- ▶ defining components of an effective mentoring relationship
- ▶ exploring potential pitfalls
- ▶ setting goals and objectives
- ▶ establishing ground rules
- ▶ identifying communication strategies
- ▶ selecting appropriate activities to meet learning objectives
- ▶ determining critical success factors.

Much depends on how formal the organization wants the mentor program to be. For more information on developing a structured, formal mentoring program, refer to ASTD's *Infoline* "Structured Mentoring: A New Approach that Works" (Thomas and Douglas, 2004).

Stretch Assignments

Stretch assignments are projects or tasks that go beyond the person's job description, go beyond the comfort zone, and enable the individual to acquire new skills as a result of the experience. Studies show that taking on difficult, challenging assignments has the most effect on developing a person's skills. These short-term assignments vary in duration, scope, and reporting relationship. The assignment may be simply job enrichment, that is, adding new challenges to the current assignment or increasing the complexity of the job. It could also involve vertical movement, upward or downward, or even horizontal, working across business units within the organization. The following are examples of stretch assignments:

- ▶ leading or implementing a new project
- ▶ organizing a conference
- ▶ leading a cross-functional team
- ▶ supervising an intern or management trainee
- ▶ researching a potential new product or an organization initiative.

Tough assignments accelerate the learning process as well as the development of one's leadership ability by requiring the individual to get out of the comfort zone and use skills that may have been used very little (or not at all) in the past.

Basic Rule 10

Stretch assignments are the most powerful individual development activities.

Job Rotation

As the name implies, leaders are assigned to work in different departments or locations as part of a rotational system. They move through a schedule of assignments that provide them with an understanding of and exposure to the entire operation. The objective of job rotation is to broaden skills. The length of time spent in each area varies depending on the individual's existing knowledge of and skill level in that area as well as the relative importance of that area to the candidate's development. The overall duration of job rotation depends on many organizational and individual factors and can last from several months to several years. Management trainee programs typically involve job rotation assignments and are supplemented by other activities and experiences, such as formal training programs, individual coaching, and monthly meetings with the program administrator and other trainees.

Networking

Networking is a supportive system of sharing information and services among individuals and groups. Networking is a process in which people and groups share information and services. Recognized as the way to get things done in today's environment, networking involves various skills and activities that rely heavily on interpersonal communication. Networking skills help the individual build a base of influence by developing strong personal and professional relationships. They may be formal or informal, inside or outside organizations. The benefits of networking can be summarized in three simple words: relationships, opportunities, and resources. Relationship building results in both personal and professional enrichment. The people you meet and who become part of your network are valuable sources of information about your industry, profession, other people, and even organizations. They are resources for gaining access to people and are a source for referrals and business leads.

Networking is an organized effort and a long-term strategy that requires work. Because networking does not come naturally to most people, potential leaders, in particular, will need help in developing their networking skills. They will also need help in understanding that networks cannot be rushed. Networks build and expand over time and need to be developed, maintained, and nurtured so that they can be activated when appropriate. Leaders should be encouraged to attend networking events inside their organizations as well as those sponsored by outside resources, such as professional and trade associations, civic and charitable organizations, and local chambers of commerce.

Loaning and Community Involvement

Some companies loan their leaders to government entities or to not-for-profit organizations to help the not-for-profit with management issues, fundraising, operations, or marketing. During the loan period, anywhere from a few months to a year, the company pays the employee's salary and benefits. One of the best-known examples of executives on loan is through United Way. In cities all across the United States, companies loan their executives to United Way to help them during their fundraising efforts. The not-for-profits certainly benefit from the knowledge and skills the corporate executive brings to the experience, and the loaned executives benefit as well. The corporate leaders learn about managing in a different environment, dealing with limited resources, and interacting with the community.

Government involvement generally takes place on the state level. Loaned executives take part in projects that focus on streamlining government services, improving processes, and saving tax dollars. In Michigan, Governor Jennifer Granholm launched an executives-on-loan program in 2003. Such programs create partnerships between the public sector and the private sector and provide a rich learning experience for the corporate leader. Earlier in his career, Edward Betof was an executive on loan to the New Jersey Governor's Commission on Quality Education, which was charged with making recommendations on improving the quality of education in the state. Speaking of his own experience, Betof said, "the assignment allowed me to step back and get a wide-angled lens of something totally different. It forced me to gain a deeper understanding of a discipline I knew only from a more limited perspective. I learned what it really means to 'give back.'" Betof emphasized that throughout the assignment "it is extremely important to stay anchored to the organization" so as not to fall into the "out-of-sight, out-of-mind" syndrome. To prevent this from happening, the organization needs to provide opportunities for the loaned executive to maintain an active connection with the company by including the employee in staff meetings and social events and communicating frequently via emails, telephone, and one-on-one meetings. The executive on loan should prepare periodic written status reports detailing what the individual is doing and the resulting personal and organizational benefits.

Leaders or high potentials might even be loaned to the organization's customers or vendors. In addition to helping the leader learn about the other organizations' operations, the experience does wonders to enhance the relationship.

Another approach is for the company to assign leaders and high potentials to serve on community boards, speak at community events, participate in fundraising efforts, or volunteer at homeless shelters. The leader develops new or enhances existing skill sets and, at the same time, begins to develop a network outside the company.

Task Forces and Process-Improvement Teams

Task forces are formed by upper management to resolve major problems immediately. Employees are temporarily excused from their regular assignments to work as task-force members. The task force is charged with developing a long-term plan to solve a problem. Often, the task force is also responsible for implementing the solution. Examples include computer conversions, new product launches, and employee reward and recognition systems. From the experience, the participant gains broader organization knowledge, develops new competencies, ties on new roles, and gets exposure to others in the organization.

Process-improvement teams are made up of experienced people from different departments or functions. Management selects the team leader and team members. Their charter is to improve the quality of products and services by improving organization-wide processes and productivity. Examples include decreasing processing time for a loan application, identifying ways to improve customer service, or implementing new security procedures.

Overseas Assignments

For global organizations, overseas assignments are becoming increasingly more important as a means of developing an organization's leaders. Overseas assignments may be part of a job rotation program. In either case, the individual is exposed to a range of tasks, jobs, and challenges. The assignment may involve introducing new technology, standardizing a process in alignment with the rest of the company, or troubleshooting. The desired outcome is a leader who has the right mix of knowledge, skills, experience, and personal attributes to lead in a global economy. An excellent leader does not necessarily make an excellent global leader. Only those with a global mindset will succeed. Developing a global mindset involves becoming culturally intelligent. Cultural intelligence "means being skilled and flexible about understanding a culture, learning more about it from your on-going interactions with it, and gradually reshaping your thinking to be more sympathetic to the culture and your behavior to be more skilled and appropriate when interacting with others from the culture" (Thomas and Inkson, 2003, 14–15).

International assignments vary according to the length of the assignment:

▶ *Short term (generally three months to one year)*. These assignments may involve supervising a project or troubleshooting.
▶ *Long term (one to five years)*. These assignments involve a clearly defined role of managing a subsidiary or business unit.

An organization can also provide high potentials with international experience by having them virtually visit the company's international sites for meetings, training programs, plant tours, short-term projects, or contractual assignments. A virtual assignment in which the leader has responsibilities for managing part of the organization in another country can be valuable as well.

Prior to any overseas assignment, the candidate must receive pre-departure training that includes the following:

▶ cultural awareness (cultural nuances such as nonverbal communication, time sense, work habits, do's and taboos, negotiation strategies, thought processes, and motivation of local employees)
▶ country awareness (employment laws, political structure, and history)
▶ etiquette and protocol (dining etiquette, gift giving, manners, and appropriate dress)
▶ language skills (learning as much as possible of the language of the host country)
▶ practical assistance (housing, entitlements, schools, job assistance for spouse or partner, expense accounts, and access to health care and other services)

▶ preliminary visits (get a feel for the business context, preview housing or schooling accommodations, how to get around, and where to shop).

It is also valuable to place potential global leaders in a business simulation as a global leader for a day. They will be challenged by various scenarios and asked to make decisions that they would encounter in a real expatriate manager situation.

Self-Directed Distance Learning Programs

For our purposes, self-directed distance learning programs refer to online courses offered by colleges and universities, trade associations, consulting firms, and organizations. Programs vary in length depending on the topic and may be credit or noncredit. Self-study may also involve a number of individual learning activities and resources, including books, articles, CD-ROMs, and the Internet.

The biggest problem with self-study programs is getting people (particularly managers) to do it. You will increase the likelihood of leaders completing self-study programs by building in mandatory assignments or methods of evaluation, such as tests, presentations, role plays, or demonstrations of new skills or behaviors. Only one thing is certain: All delivery methods (including traditional classroom) will change and evolve with the growing development of technology.

When you design web-based training and other distance learning programs, follow the same principles of good instructional design that you would for classroom learning. One of the important elements of learning lost in many of the distance learning delivery modes, web-based training in particular, is the loss of nonverbal communication and interaction. Because many people have a need to exchange ideas, opinions, and viewpoints, the designer needs to build in opportunities for learners to interact with the instructor and with each other. There are many ways to add the human touch: bulletin boards, threaded discussions, chat rooms, email, and audio or video conferencing.

Noted

Unless there is a strong psychological reason for completing a learning task, only about 20 percent will be motivated to start and only half of that will finish the intended e-learning.

Advantages of Self-Directed Distance Learning

The use of self-directed distance learning can be very helpful to organizations that seek to bridge the learning-delivery gaps caused by multiple geographic locations, time constraints, and other barriers to learning. The following is an overview of the many benefits of self-directed distance learning:

▶ **Easy Access**. Learners can access the course material at their convenience and when and where they need it. This is particularly important for people who work at remote locations, are on the road a great deal, or just have busy schedules.

▶ **Cost Savings**. Traditional classroom-based courses are expensive. In addition to the cost involved with the training room and its associated overhead costs, distance learning saves travel costs.

▶ **More Efficient**. In addition to being economical, distance learning allows you to deliver training to a large number of people at multiple sites at the same time. This is particularly important when an organization with multiple sites is rolling out a new product or process that needs to be introduced to all employees at the same time. Think about how long it would take (and how costly) to train several hundred people on a new product.

▶ **Timeliness**. For training to be effective, it must take place as close as possible to when the learner is actually going to use the knowledge or skills.

▶ **Learner-Centered**. Learners are in control of their own learning. They can access the material or segments of material they really need and bypass or review those that they already know. They can spend more time on or revisit content without feeling rushed or pressured. Learners can also start and stop when they need to accommodate their schedules.

▶ **Links Employees**. With growing globalization, technology-based distance learning enables people from different locations throughout the world to connect and learn from each other.

▶ **Consistency**. Because the content is being delivered from a central source, there is consistency in what the learners see and hear.

▶ **Better Use of Experts**. Subject matter experts' time can be used more effectively and efficiently, particularly when they can choose when and how their expertise will be made available to learners rather than be at the mercy of a specific classroom-based time and location.

Disadvantages of Self-Directed Distance Learning

No delivery mode is perfect, and distance learning has its drawbacks as well. The following list describes the most frequently cited disadvantages of distance learning:

- ▶ **Learner's Experience with Technology.** One of the first obstacles one needs to overcome in implementing technology-based distance learning is the technophobic learner. Some people may be unfamiliar with the technology and will require extra time and training to bring them up to speed. Still others may be resistant because their overwhelming workload prevents them from spending the time to complete self-directed courses or participate in real-time seminars.

- ▶ **Available Technology.** Although technology and its capabilities are advancing rapidly, not all people and organizations are keeping up with it. Some organizations may be on the cutting edge while others may be several iterations behind in software or hardware capabilities. Existing technology may be inadequate. For example, the system may not have enough bandwidth to run some graphics programs or the new software needed to deliver a program may not be compatible with the hardware. Not all employees may have access to the Internet.

- ▶ **Reduced Social and Cultural Interaction**. What is often missing in the technology-based sessions is the peer-to-peer interaction and learning opportunities that contribute to team building and relationship building. However, as communication technologies continue to advance, this perceived barrier will diminish somewhat.

- ▶ **Does Not Appeal to All Learning Styles.** People who have a need for face-to-face interaction will have a difficult time embracing distance learning. It simply does not fit with their learning styles. We know that learning styles are important to consider, and technology-based learning does not fit the needs of those whose learning preferences lean heavily on group interaction.

- ▶ **Up-Front Investment.** While distance learning may be cost-effective in the long run, it requires a substantial up-front investment in development costs, hardware, and software.

- ▶ **Not All Subjects Are Appropriate**. Technology-based courses heavily focused on cognitive learning are the best candidates for the various modes of e-learning. Also, skills (behavioral learning domain) can be taught through simulations and other interactive designs. Affective learning is much more difficult to address in technology-based learning because of the need for human interaction.

▶ **More Cumbersome**. More collaboration and teamwork are needed for distance learning because more people are involved. Traditional classroom training primarily involves an instructional designer, course developer, and facilitator/trainer. In many cases, these roles may be assigned to one person. In developing distance learning, you need to include technology experts, distance site facilitators, and facilities support.

Miscellaneous Individual Development Experiences

In addition to the many individual leadership development activities discussed in this chapter, below are some other options you may want to consider for certain individuals, depending on their specific needs.

A New Position

When you want an individual to develop certain skills and options such as job rotation are not possible, you may want to create an entirely new position for that person. The new position, of course, must fill a specific need for the organization as well. For example, your organization may have reached a point where you need a director of professional development or a regional sales manager.

Interim or Temporary Assignment

When a vacancy occurs, particularly if it is unexpected, you may be scrambling to find a replacement. One way to solve the problem for the organization and also create a great development opportunity for the high-potential employee is to assign that individual to fill that vacancy until you can find a permanent replacement. In many cases, the person who is in the acting manager position eventually becomes the official replacement.

Job Swap

Job swapping for a short period of time can be very helpful in giving people a broader perspective on other areas in the organization that are related to theirs. For example, an individual in sales might job swap with someone in marketing or a high potential in customer service would exchange positions with an employee in research and development. Not only would those involved benefit from learning about the functions and responsibilities of another department, but also the experience and interaction can be instrumental in breaking down silos within the organization.

Internal Short-Term Experiences

The following short-term activities can be used to supplement other assignments or positions in which the individual is engaged:

- ▶ represent the organization at a conference or professional association meeting
- ▶ conduct a study
- ▶ facilitate a training session
- ▶ develop a new process
- ▶ participate on a cross-functional team
- ▶ chair a company-sponsored event
- ▶ write a white paper on a topic related to your business
- ▶ develop a new training program
- ▶ mentor someone in another area
- ▶ write a proposal for a new project or initiative.

External Short-Term Experiences

The following external activities can be valuable in helping the individual develop interpersonal, leadership, and business skills and also give exposure to other business models. At the same time, the individual will be developing networking relationships:

- ▶ visit a customer's or supplier's site
- ▶ attend a customer's convention
- ▶ speak at a vendor's meeting or conference
- ▶ chair a United Way fundraising campaign
- ▶ facilitate a strategic planning session for a charitable or professional organization
- ▶ get involved with a community or professional organization
- ▶ serve on a board
- ▶ write an article for a professional publication
- ▶ become active in the local Chamber of Commerce with activities such as "Business Volunteers for the Arts" or "Business on Board."

Short-Term External Training or Executive Education

To supplement the internal development activities, sometimes individuals need additional knowledge acquisition that may be available only through an outside source, such as a college or university. These courses or programs need to be carefully chosen so that they meet the needs of both the individual and the organization.

Think About This

To gain interest in and support for individual learning activities, publicize the names of those who have completed a particular program and perhaps include their comments about the positive outcomes they have experienced as a result.

Getting It Done

Make a list of all the individual development activities discussed in this chapter plus others that you may have thought of yourself. Include the list with any materials and written communication you send to leaders and high potentials. It will help them when they prepare their individual development plans in collaboration with their managers.

In the next chapter, you will learn about the various external experiences and resources that you may choose to be a part of your overall leadership development program.

7

External Leadership Programs

What's Inside This Chapter

In this chapter, you'll learn

▶ About university programs
▶ The role of outside resources
▶ How to select outside resources.

More and more, organizations are reaching out and forming partnerships with external resources, such as colleges and universities, trade associations, and consulting firms, to supplement internal leadership development programs. These programs range from intensive mini-MBA programs to topic-specific seminars lasting several days to several weeks and even months. The classes are held at the provider's site and are attended by people from various organizations and levels within those organizations. Let's take a look at some of the specific sources and types of programs outside the organization.

Noted

The trend in external executive education offerings is away from longer programs to shorter, more targeted programs that supplement an organization's overall leadership development initiative.

Universities and Colleges

Traditional universities and colleges continue to be the source for those seeking advance degrees such as MBAs. Leaders at all levels are seeing the benefits of earning MBAs as aids to career advancement.

Out of necessity, business schools are beginning to adapt to meet new needs. As companies become more global and the need for global leadership skills intensifies, business schools are putting more emphasis on an international focus. For example, many are forming alliances with universities abroad. Several schools are also creating a closer connection between how business is taught and how careers are evolving. For example, at Pepperdine's Graziadio School of Business and Management, students work on marketing problems brought by companies such as Disney and Coca-Cola. Recognizing the working professional's busy schedule and the need to balance work and family while working on a degree, colleges and universities offer many options to fit a variety of lifestyles.

Degree Programs

Colleges and universities offer both undergraduate and graduate programs in a variety of formats, well-suited to today's busy professional. The following are descriptions of the various options available to those seeking degrees:

- ▶ *Traditional Night School Classes.* These programs follow a traditional education model in which students attend class one or two nights a week and can expect to receive their degrees in three or four years.
- ▶ *Executive MBA Programs.* These programs tend to cater to higher-level leaders within an organization. Classes are normally held on Friday nights, Saturdays, and Sundays so that executives do not lose any precious work time during the week. In most cases, students in executive MBA programs

are part of a cohort, that is, a learning group of 15 to 18 people that remains intact over the period of time it takes to complete the degree requirements.

▶ *Accelerated Programs.* These programs are similar to the executive MBA programs in that they follow a cohort model. Students move through the program in groups of 18 to 25 and attend class once a week in evening sessions. The length of an accelerated program varies with the academic institution but is generally 18 to 24 months. Students are required to have some work experience for admission. They may have direct management responsibility.

▶ *Online Programs.* More and more universities are offering degrees online. Online degree programs offer convenience and flexibility enabling learners to fit their education pursuits around busy work and personal schedules. This option is particularly appealing to those who travel a lot because the learning can occur at any place or time, as long as the learner has access to a computer and the Internet.

▶ *Non-Traditional Universities.* Non-traditional for-profit organizations, such as the University of Phoenix, Kaplan, Capella, and Strayer, are known primarily for their online degree programs, although many of them have "campus" locations in cities across the country.

▶ *Interactive Distance Learning.* This option is truly a blended learning design. Students learn through a mix of independent study and structured course work; learn peer to peer or collaboratively with faculty; and use a variety of learning media including online courses, face-to-face classes, seminars, and email. The Fielding Institute, located in Santa Barbara, California, is known for its blended learning approach in which students create their own curricula, and the faculty serves as mentors throughout the learning process.

Non-Degree Programs

Employers often use non-degree programs to supplement or augment their leadership development initiatives. These may be structured leadership programs with set curricula or shorter, stand-alone classes addressing a particular topic.

Executive Education Programs

The majority of top-ranking universities with business schools offer executive education programs, and an increasing number of smaller colleges and universities are getting into the business as well. Prominent universities offering leadership development programs include the Wharton School at the University of Pennsylvania, Stanford University, the University of Michigan, Penn State University, Columbia University, and Stanford University. More and more of these educational institutions are customizing their offerings for specific companies.

Short, Open-Enrollment Leadership Programs

A need still exists for short, open-enrollment courses sponsored by universities. These courses range from one or two days to a few weeks. They can be effective in helping high potentials gain knowledge in particular areas as preparation for a new assignment in the organization or to enhance a basic understanding of a particular responsibility. For example, someone who is asked to lead a project for the first time may need a short course in project management.

Training Resource Organizations

In addition to universities, private organizations such as the Center for Creative Leadership (CCL), a not-for-profit organization headquartered in Greensboro, North Carolina, offer both open-enrollment and organization-specific leadership programs. CCL programs are rich and intense and are based on solid and extensive research. Also, companies that have their own very successful internal leadership programs are now offering to share their leadership principles and practices with the rest of the world. One notable example is the Disney Institute that offers a program on the Disney Approach to Leadership Excellence. Programs offered through these types of organizations are generally residential and vary in length from several days to several weeks.

Off-Site Retreats and Experiential Activities

Off-site retreats involve taking a group of leaders from the same organization and immersing them in a learning experience for several days at a conference center or other facility away from the work site. Most often these experiences focus on promoting teamwork or provide an opportunity to address specific issues, roles, or processes. For intense team-building experiences, organizations sometimes turn to outdoor experiential-learning programs that involve some type of physical activity such as rock climbing, river rafting, or ropes courses. Off-site retreats are often used as a precursor to the formalized internal classroom sessions.

For those less adventurous, other experiential programs (conducted inside or outside) provide hands-on problem-solving tasks that have individuals and groups improving their leadership and team skills. As with computer simulations, people are encouraged to try new behaviors in a nonthreatening environment. These activities are typically conducted in a shorter timeframe of three to four hours, although some can last several days and are conducted by the consulting company's facilitators. VisionPoint Consulting (www.visionpointconsulting.com) is a good source for both indoor and outdoor experiential activities. Other sources are CEO Chef (www.ceochef.com) and Teambonding (www.teambonding.com). For organizations that want to use experiential activities as part of a particular leadership module but do not want the expense of bringing in an outside company, HRDQ (www.hrdq.com) is an excellent resource. The Mars Surface Rover is one example of an activity that teaches facilitative leadership skills.

To be effective, all simulations and experiential activities must be integrated into the leadership development program. In all cases, the true learning takes place during the debriefing or processing phase of the experience.

Basic Rule 11

The quality of the facilitation is the key to success with any experiential program. A good facilitator will spend a significant amount of time debriefing or processing the activity, prodding the participants to reflect on the learning experience and how they are going to apply it to their work environment.

Trade and Professional Associations

Many trade and professional associations have their own education programs. In many cases, they partner with traditional colleges and universities and use a combination of professionals in their field as well as university professors.

The American Bankers Association (ABA), the largest banking trade association in the United States, is an excellent example of a trade association with an extensive and comprehensive professional development program. The ABA Stonier Graduate School of Banking is the preeminent executive management school for the financial services industry. The structure includes three one-week residential sessions (one per year) with projects and papers between sessions plus the completion of a capstone strategic project. The program is conducted on the campus of the University of Pennsylvania. In addition to this premier program for bank leaders, the association offers a multitude of professional education programs in the areas of lending, retail and business banking, wealth management, and compliance. The sessions are offered in various venues (online, face-to-face, webcasts, teleseminars), and many are part of a diploma or certificate program. The ABA also offers customized in-house programs for its members.

The American Society for Training & Development (ASTD), the leading association of workplace learning and performance professionals, offers a certification, the Certified Professional in Learning and Performance, through the ASTD Certification Institute.

The Society for Human Resource Management (SHRM) is another good example of a professional association that offers a wide range of educational programs. SHRM is the world's largest professional association devoted to human resource management. Its educational offerings include many workshops, seminars, conferences, and a certification component. The Human Resource Certification Institute is the leading independent, internationally recognized certifying body for the human resource profession.

Selection Criteria

Before recommending or selecting an external resource for a group or an individual, make sure you do your homework. You want to make sure that the program and the provider are aligned with the needs of the individual involved as well as the organization. Develop a list of criteria you will use to select the best option. The following are some things you may want to consider as you evaluate the multitude of offerings available:

- ▶ What are the needs of the organization that the course or program will address?
- ▶ What are the needs of the individual that the course or program will address?
- ▶ What is the length of the program, and is it compatible with the participant's availability?
- ▶ What is the reputation of the provider and the instructors?

- Who else will be attending? What companies do they represent, and what are their positions within their companies?
- What type of program is it: degree, certificate, certification?
- What delivery methods will be used, and are they aligned with the participant's learning style, lifestyle, and available time?
- What is the cost of the program?
- How will the effectiveness be measured?

Think About This

An instructor can make or break a program. Be sure to check references for the organization offering the program as well as the instructor teaching it. Also, check on class size. Some seminars are designed for large groups (over 50), resulting in little or no opportunity for meaningful group interaction or skill-building activities. Above all else, you must consider the program's relevance to the organization's business challenges and make sure you are clear about the reason you are having the person take the course or participate in the program.

Getting It Done

Make a list of all of the external development programs that are available to the people in your organization. For each one, develop a list of pros and cons based on the criteria presented in this chapter.

In the next chapter, you are going to learn how to evaluate the effectiveness of your program using Kirkpatrick's four-level model of evaluation.

8

Program Evaluation:
The Four Levels

■ ■

What's Inside This Chapter

In this chapter, you'll learn

▶ The four levels of evaluation
▶ How to design evaluation tools
▶ About the evaluation process.

In good times, but especially in bad times, there is and will continue to be an emphasis on proving the value of training. Measuring the effect of training and other development activities becomes even more critical and difficult when the evaluation process applies to a leadership development program. The purpose of this chapter is to provide an overview of the four-level model of evaluation developed by Donald Kirkpatrick ("The Four Levels of Evaluation," *Infoline*, 2007).

Why Evaluate?

Evaluation is an ongoing process, not just something that happens at the end of a session, activity, or program. Consider evaluation during the session, at the end, and after the participants return to the job.

The methods used in evaluation are pretty much the same as those used to gather data during the needs assessment (as described in chapter 4). Evaluation needs to be a part of every development activity or experience.

Four-Level Model for Training Evaluation

The most widely known model for evaluating training programs was introduced by Donald Kirkpatrick in 1959. It is regarded as a classic by workplace learning practitioners. Although all four levels of the model (reaction, learning, behavior, results) are important, you may choose not to evaluate at all four levels. Studies show that a vast majority of organizations evaluate reaction. A significantly high percentage of companies measure learning as well. The evaluation of behavior lags behind the first two levels, with Level 4 finishing last; however, as organizations become increasingly more cost conscious, the need to measure the effectiveness of training and development will continue to grow. Table 8-1 provides an overview of the four levels of evaluation.

Level 1: Reaction

Level 1 deals with participant reaction, that is, customer satisfaction. Level 1 evaluations are often referred to as smile sheets, implying that participants' reactions are based on how much fun they had in the training session. For that reason, learning leaders frequently dismiss Level 1 evaluations as a waste of time.

On the contrary, Level 1 is an important first step in determining the success of a training program. Participants' reactions can help you determine the effectiveness of a program and how it can be improved. If the participants have a bad experience, they will certainly communicate their dissatisfaction, which, in turn, will affect how well key decision makers support the program.

What Level 1 Can't Measure

One of the problems with and the main cause of criticism of Level 1 evaluation is that it is too subjective and often becomes nothing more than a popularity contest. Before you start constructing a participant end-of-session evaluation form, you

Table 8-1. Measuring Training Results.

	What	Who	When	How	Why
Level 1	Reaction Did they like it?	Participants	End of program	Smile sheets	Determine level of customer satisfaction May indicate need for revision
Level 2	Learning What knowledge or skills did they retain?	Participants Trainer	Before, during, and after program	Pretest/posttest Skills application through role plays, case studies, exercises	Identify if trainer has been successful in delivery of course content and achieving program objectives
Level 3	Behavior How are they performing differently?	Participants Bosses Subordinates Peers	Three to six months after program completion	Surveys Interviews Observations Performance appraisals	Determine extent to which they have transferred what they learned in the classroom to the actual work situation
Level 4	Results What is the effect on the bottom line?	Participants Control group	After completion of Level 3 follow-up	Cost-benefit analysis Tracking Operational data	Determine if benefits outweigh costs Ascertain degree of contribution of program to organizational goals

must first understand what it cannot and is not intended to do. It does not measure learning or the ability to apply learning on the job. It also cannot measure changes in attitudes or beliefs. Because this level deals only with participants' perceptions and reactions, a Level 1 instrument can in no way measure organizational impact. Although frequently found as a specific line item on participant sheets, participants cannot measure the trainer's knowledge. They can, however, evaluate the trainer's ability to communicate or demonstrate knowledge.

Deciding What to Measure

Before you design a Level 1 instrument, you need to be clear about what you want to know and why you want to know it. Also, what are you going to do with the information? Don't ask for information about something you can't change or have no intention of analyzing or reporting.

Designing an End-of-Session Evaluation Form

Evaluation forms are difficult to construct. You should find the following guidelines helpful when you begin working on your own evaluation:

▶ Keep the form brief. Participants should be able to complete it quickly.
▶ Create a balance among the various types of information you are collecting. For example, don't ask five questions about the instructor and only two about content.
▶ Get 100 percent immediate reaction. In other words, have participants complete the evaluation before they leave the room. This will ensure that you get feedback from everyone. It will also prevent mob mentality response, that is, the possibility of several people getting together to discuss the class either before or while they are completing the evaluation.

Categories. You must first decide what you want to measure and create questions or response items that address or fall into certain categories. These categories will include many, if not all, of the following:

▶ Content—Was the content practical? Did it meet the participants' needs?
▶ Materials—How useful were the learning materials?
▶ Instructional Methods—How effective were the activities and exercises? Did the trainer use a variety of methods?

▶ Trainer—How effective was the trainer in communicating the information, facilitating a discussion, or engaging the group?

▶ Environment—How comfortable was the learning environment?

You will also want to get the participants' perceptions of how valuable the experience was and how they will apply what they learned. Questions such as, "What was the most important thing you learned?" and "What are you going to do, do differently, or stop doing as a result of this training?" will help you determine the value the participants received as a result of the learning experience.

It is also a good idea to provide an opportunity for participants to make recommendations as to how the program can be improved and also to express their overall reactions to the session.

Format. To counteract people's tendency to respond the same way to every item on a questionnaire, use a variety of response formats. Choose at least four from the following options:

▶ Two-choice questions with room for explanations or comments. These would include responses such as "yes" or "no" and "agree" or "disagree." Example: Did the course meet the stated objectives? Yes_____No_____

▶ Short answers. These items are written as open-ended questions and require the respondent to write down a brief response instead of just checking a box. Example: What parts of the workshop were most valuable/beneficial to you? Why?

▶ Complete the sentence. With this item, the respondent is asked to complete a sentence. Example: What I want/need to know more about is . . .

▶ Ratings. Participants respond to a question or statement using some type of scale or rating, such as the Likert scale. The Likert scale measures both the direction (positive to negative) and intensity (strongly positive to strongly negative) of an individual's opinion or attitude. Example: Today's session was an enjoyable and satisfying learning experience for me.

1	2	3	4	5	6	7	8
Strongly Disagree			Agree			Strongly Agree	

▶ Rankings. This item asks respondents to indicate priorities or preferences. Example: Please rank each topic in order of its importance or relevance to your job. 1 = most important, 5 = least important.

▶ Checklist. A checklist provides a laundry list from which participants can choose words that express their reactions. Example: Check the words that describe your reaction to today's session:

    _____Exceeded my expectations

    _____Met my expectations

    _____Fell short of my expectations

You can also add a question focusing on the effect of the session on the participants and designed to obtain a deeper and more personal response than a questionnaire would elicit. Example: Imagine that a co-worker (or friend) of yours is thinking about attending this program. He or she asks you, "What was this program like for you?" How do you respond?

Basic Rule 12
You should use Level 1 evaluation (reaction sheets) for all programs.

Interviews

In addition to the end-of-session questionnaires, you should use interviews to increase the reliability of the data collected from the questionnaires. Interviews can be very helpful in evaluating a leadership development program. This method of data collection is quite flexible, allowing the interviewer to probe for more specific answers and to clarify questions as needed. The method also allows the interviewer to record spontaneous answers and, therefore, get a more complete picture of the participants' reactions. The interviewer can explore in more detail the reactions gleaned from the questionnaires.

Plan on spending about 30 minutes per interview. In practical terms, you will not be able to interview every participant. Select a random sample of participants to interview. It is important to hold the interviews within one week of the session so that the experience is fresh in the participants' minds. Through one-on-one interviews, you can further explore the reasons for participants' reactions and solicit suggestions for improvement. You can either tape the interviews and have them transcribed, allowing you to analyze or interpret the responses more thoroughly, or take notes during the interview.

When developing the interview questions, do not duplicate the questions on the written form. Instead, ask specific questions about the methods used or the content covered. For example, below are several questions you might ask about the leadership development program:

- ▶ What did you like about the action learning projects?
- ▶ What was the biggest challenge in the action learning projects?
- ▶ What activity or experience was most beneficial to you?
- ▶ How do you expect this experience to enhance your leadership skills?

Think About This

Think about what you want to know about the participants' reactions to the overall leadership development program or just the training component. Then design a form that will quantify reactions.

Level 2: Learning

Level 2 evaluation deals with learning. Learning refers to the knowledge (cognitive domain), skills (behavioral domain), and attitudes (affective domain). Of these three learning domains, affective is the most challenging to evaluate. It is far easier to determine what new knowledge or skills the participants acquired than the ways in which the training changed their opinions, values, and beliefs.

Essentially, Level 2 measures the effectiveness of the instructor. In a leadership development program, the quality of the instruction is paramount. If participants have not learned, they certainly cannot be expected to change behavior.

The two most appropriate methods used to evaluate learning are tests and observations.

Tests

One type of testing involves using standardized assessments related to a specific topic that you may purchase from a publisher. An example would be an inventory that addresses delegation practices. Many trainers administer tests before and after training. The difference between pretest and posttest results provides a fairly accurate measurement of knowledge and attitudes. Another type of testing is company specific. Some leadership development programs include training sessions that deal with factual information such as policies, procedures, and laws. Organizations that have a specific knowledge base they expect their leaders and high potentials to master should develop their own tests. Developing test or quiz questions is not easy.

Types of Tests. You must first determine whether you want to construct subjective (short answer or essay) or objective (multiple choice or true-false) items or even a combination of the two types. When constructing test items, you need to consider the time needed to grade the test as well as the validity and reliability of each item. Make sure the test assesses the learning as specified in the learning objectives. When an item measures what it is supposed to measure, it has validity. Each test item must also be reliable, that is, giving consistent results from one application to another.

Make sure the test is meaningful. Instead of asking for simple information or factual recall, ask questions that require the participants to apply or interpret what they learned in the session.

Test-Writing Guidelines. In most cases, you will probably choose to develop multiple-choice questions. They are easy to grade, but not necessarily easy to write. To help you construct a multiple-choice test that will provide valuable information about the participant's content mastery, consider the following guidelines:

- ▶ avoid "all of the above" and "none of the above" in your set of answer options
- ▶ make sure the stem (that is, the main part of the question) contains most of the information and defines the problem and place missing words near the end
- ▶ maintain grammatical consistency or parallel structure for both the stem and the answer choices
- ▶ try to create choices of equal length
- ▶ avoid ambiguity and reading difficulty by stating questions in the positive rather than in the negative

▶ keep the sentence stem simple and limit it to one idea

▶ use conversational language when phrasing the item and its choices

▶ arrange the questions in logical order

▶ do not give clues to the correct answer in the question.

Question Formats. All multiple-choice questions consist of a stem and a response. The stem presents a problem, asks a question, or takes the form of an incomplete statement. Responses include possible answers, all of which must be plausible. The greater the number of items, the better the test's reliability. Following are some formats to consider:

▶ *Correct Answer.* The correct answer format asks a simple question to which there is only one correct answer. It is used primarily to test the recall of straight facts. This type of question is appropriate to test product knowledge.

▶ *Best Answer.* With this type of question, there is more than one correct choice. Some or all of the choices may be correct to some degree. The best-answer question requires a higher level of thinking, expecting the responder to truly evaluate the choices and draw conclusions. This type of question can create many problems. Because it is open to interpretation, the test item can be challenged quite easily, and you might find yourself either arguing with the individual or group and most probably having to give credit for other answers.

▶ *Combined Response.* This question is the most complicated and time consuming for both the test writer and the test taker. The choices, one or more that may be correct, are numbered. Then there is a second set of choices that list combinations of possible correct responses. This type of question assesses complex cognitive skills and the ability to analyze and evaluate. You must exercise a great deal of thought when writing the item, and, because of its complexity, the respondent will probably have to spend more time thinking about the item before responding.

The test formats described so far measure a change in knowledge or attitude. To evaluate an increase in skills, you will need to conduct a performance test. For example, if you are conducting a program on "Conducting Effective Meetings," you would ask each participant to facilitate a brief segment of a mock meeting at the beginning of the program. You would critique each participant's performance and assign a grade or point value. During the program, you would communicate the principles and techniques for facilitating an effective meeting. Toward the end of the program, each participant would again facilitate a short segment and receive another critique and evaluation. If the training has been successful, each participant's performance score will have improved.

Observations

One of the best ways to evaluate learning in a leadership development program is through observation. Trainers can watch participants practicing and applying skills, tools, and techniques during the session. As the trainers observe participant behavior in skill practices, role plays, simulations, case studies, and other activities, they can get a good idea of what the participants have really learned. For example, in a session dealing with group decision making and problem solving, you would put participants in teams of five to seven people. The teams would work together in a challenging paper-and-pencil survival simulation during which they have an opportunity to put consensus decision making into practice. HRDQ (www.HRDQ.com), Pfeiffer (www.Pfeiffer.com), and Human Synergistics (www.humansyn.com) are excellent resources for adventure-type simulations.

Basic Rule 13
If the learner hasn't learned, the teacher hasn't taught.

Level 3: Behavior

The critical question answered by Level 3 is, "How has the training affected the way participants perform on the job?" Although both line managers and learning leaders agree that the success of a training program is determined by what the participants do with the information or skills back on the job, these results are often ignored. Level 3 evaluation is both time consuming and costly. It also requires good organizational and follow-up skills and processes.

Follow-Up Guidelines

Prepare participants for the follow-up evaluation. Participants need to understand clearly that a change in behavior is not only desired but also expected. At the end of the training session, tell participants that you will be conducting a follow-up evaluation and what type of evaluation it will be. This is where the leadership competencies assessment can be extremely helpful.

In chapter 3, we suggested the use of an Individual Needs Assessment (table 3-1) to identify the skill level of various leadership competencies. You may recall this assessment is most effective when both participants and their managers complete the assessment and then discuss it prior to the formal training program. The open and honest dialogue should indicate the specific competencies the participant needs to improve. In so doing, the assessment then provides a baseline against which to measure or evaluate the participant following the training or experience. For the assessment to be effective, the participant must have an opportunity to use the new behavior. In other words, two or three months after the experience, each participant and manager should repeat the evaluation, then once again meet to discuss the results, comparing the self-evaluation to the manager's evaluation, noting areas of similarity and disagreement, and focusing on the changes in behavior as indicated by the response.

If the training wasn't effective, find out why. Encourage participants to identify reasons why they haven't improved and what factors obstructed their progress. Sometimes unknown factors inhibit or prevent the application of the new knowledge and skills on the job. These barriers might include poor environmental conditions, lack of proper equipment, the supervisor, existing policies and procedures, or even the organizational climate.

These results should be shared with the leadership development administrator who will then report the findings and conclusions to senior management.

If you used 360-degree feedback, you may want to repeat that process after a significant amount of time has elapsed and the participant has had ample opportunity to change behavior or apply skills learned through the training or other experiences.

Interviews

Not only should you interview those who went through the training, but you also want to interview those who are affected by or closely associated with the program participants. Possible interviewees include the participants' managers, co-workers, customers, or subordinates.

The interview questions would have to be carefully constructed and designed to focus on specific applications and behavior changes.

Noted

In a patterned interview on behavior change, all interviewees are asked the same questions. You then tabulate responses to create quantitative data.

Regardless of which evaluation method(s) you use, make sure you allow enough time for the behavior change to take place. The length of time depends on the program, but three to six months should give the participants ample opportunity to apply what they learned and develop new behaviors.

Surveys

Surveys are a more efficient and less expensive way to find out if the participants are actually applying what they learned. Once again, don't limit your sources of information. Others who interact with those who participated in the training are often a more reliable source of feedback. You will want to know not only if trainees are using the training on the job but also how they're using it to perform better.

Level 4: Results

Level 4 evaluation determines the effect of the leadership development program on the organization. Ideally, it shows how the program has contributed to accomplishing organizational goals and objectives. This level focuses on business results. If an organization chooses to conduct a Level 4 evaluation, the area of measurement must be the same as that identified in the needs assessment.

To measure the program's effect on the bottom line, you will need to return to the data gathered during the needs assessment. In other words, you must determine your critical success factors up front. Results you wish to measure could include any of the following:

▶ production output
▶ sales
▶ operating costs
▶ customer satisfaction
▶ quality standards

- safety record
- turnover rate
- absenteeism
- employee grievances
- employee satisfaction
- budget variances
- promotions.

To adequately measure specific factors, the organization must have good records on whatever the areas of measurement are to be. Because situations can change so rapidly, you will need to repeat the Level 4 evaluation periodically as determined by senior management. For example, an employee opinion survey or an employee engagement survey can yield valuable information on leadership behaviors.

Level 4 evaluation is difficult because of the many variables that can come into play. This is particularly true for leadership development. For example, variables that could affect turnover might be demographic shifts or changes in benefits. Again, be very clear up front what results you expect to see and also be aware that the improvements will lag behind the changes in behavior (Level 3).

Evaluating E-Learning Experiences

Unlike traditional evaluations, e-learning evaluations are somewhat difficult because of delivery options and individual learning solutions that often prevent consistency and uniformity in the evaluation process. For example, not all learners will complete self-study courses from start to finish. Some will choose only the modules they think they need. Others may have to go back and repeat a module to gain a greater understanding of its content.

For the most part, however, you can apply the same principles and strategies of traditional evaluation methods and levels as discussed throughout this chapter to the e-learning process. The basic difference, of course, is that the various evaluation methods will be done electronically. The following are types of evaluations that can be adapted to an e-learning environment.

Level 1 evaluation measures participants' reactions. Methods that can be used include questionnaires completed on-screen within the course or as email feedback. Participant reactions can also be captured via online focus groups or in chat rooms.

Level 2, which measures what participants actually learned, uses various tests. Almost all types of tests can be adapted to an electronic format: true-false, multiple choice, essay, fill-in-the-blanks, matching. Visit William Horton's website (www .horton.com) for great examples of various testing formats. In addition to testing, you can monitor learners by observing their behaviors in learning activities such as simulations and learning games, as well as role plays conducted in chat rooms.

To evaluate how well participants apply what they learned (Level 3), you would turn to traditional methods such as observations of the employees' on-the-job performance, surveys completed by the participants and others who interact with them, and job performance records. It might also be appropriate to set up control groups: Some employees would experience traditional classroom-based training while others would engage in e-learning activities. Employees' individual action plans could also be monitored.

Level 4 evaluation for distance learning is much the same as it is for traditional learning and would involve determining return-on-investment (ROI), as well as determining benefits such as a decrease in the number of accidents, safety violations, tardiness, absenteeism, turnover, customer complaints, and grievances. Business metrics such as profitability (sales, revenues, profit) and financial health (stock price, market share) might also be targeted for Level 4 evaluation.

As with any evaluation process, it is important to collaborate with the organization's leaders to determine the success criteria. What specifically do the key people want to measure, and how will they use the information?

Getting It Done

To validate the results of your evaluations, choose a control group of employees (those who did not receive the training) from the same function as the program participants. Ask members of the control group to complete the same surveys, questionnaires, and tests as those completed by the participants. Monitor the control group's performance, and compare it with that of the employees who received training.

In the next chapter, you will learn how to determine the bottom-line impact of a leadership development program.

Determining the Impact of Leadership Development

What's Inside This Chapter

In this chapter, you'll learn

▶ The relationship between needs assessment and evaluation
▶ About various ROI methods of evaluation.

As competitive pressures increase and profit margins shrink, leadership development expenses will be more closely scrutinized. As a result, quantifying the impact of the investment in leadership development will be a major priority.

Measuring the total impact of a leadership development program is both challenging and time consuming. Considering the complexities and intangible and tangible variables, most organizations are more than satisfied if they are able to conduct a Level 4 evaluation. To those who are charged with proving that the cost of a leadership development program is well worth the investment, this chapter provides an overview of the various approaches to a Level 5 evaluation.

Basic Rule 14
Effective training must be driven by business results.

The Critical Link: Needs Assessment and Evaluation

As discussed in chapter 4, needs assessment is critical to the success of any training and development initiative. It provides the basis for program development and establishes the criteria for measuring the success of the program after its completion. For evaluation to have any meaning, it must be tied to the needs assessment process. In other words, you must determine at the very beginning what you want to measure. What are the critical success factors that will determine the overall effectiveness of the program? As a learning leader, you will determine the metrics in collaboration with the senior management team who will determine which metrics to incorporate into the leadership development program. These metrics should be tied directly to the strategic plan.

Think About This

Return to your needs assessment and make sure it is aligned with what you want to measure. Also, make sure you have the mechanisms in place to capture quantifiable data.

Accountability for Training

Throughout the business world, accountability of all functions is increasing. Staff functions such as training are now expected to prove their contribution and value to the organization. Top executives are demanding that training departments offer proof of their worth or take budget cuts. Should you be asked to justify the time, effort, and money spent on training, below is a brief overview of two approaches to measurement: (1) return-on-investment and (2) cost-benefit analysis.

Return-on-Investment Approach

The ROI simply shows what the payback is for the program. You are comparing monetary benefits with program benefits. To determine ROI, you must wait three to

Noted

A comprehensive return-on-investment process will probably not cost more than four to five percent of the overall training and human resource development budget.

six months and even longer for operational results. If training programs fail to show a reasonable return on the company's investment, future (or even current) training initiatives are at risk.

Level 5 evaluation (ROI) is an extension of Kirkpatrick's four-level model of evaluation. The ROI process model developed by Jack Phillips takes Level 4 to another level. The following is a brief overview of the model.

Step One: Collect Post-Program Data

ROI (Level 5) uses Levels 4 and 5 data that include hard data (output, quality, cost, time) and soft data (work climate, attitudes). The data collection methods are the same as discussed in chapter 8.

Because leadership development is an ongoing process, you should conduct an ROI analysis at regular intervals based on how extensive your program is. If your program consists primarily of a series of structured training programs, then conduct the analysis after the series is complete. If you have included other development experiences, you may choose to conduct an analysis of those experiences separately or as part of the overall program.

Step Two: Isolate the Effects of Training

In this step, you are exploring the output performance directly related to the program. To do so, you should use a variety and combination of techniques to isolate the effects of training. These techniques include using a control group, trend line analysis, forecasting model, and impact estimates. For more details and an explanation of these methods, refer to *Infoline*, "Level 5 Evaluation: ROI," by Jack Phillips (1998).

Step Three: Convert Data to Monetary Value

In step 3, you will use Level 4 data, convert them to monetary values, and compare them with program costs. Again, a number of techniques are available depending on the data available and what you are trying to accomplish.

Step Four: Tabulate Program Costs

The last step deals with determining the costs related to the program. This would include designing and developing, program materials, instructor salary, facilities, participant salaries, travel expenses, and administration. Due to the extensive nature of a leadership development program, you would probably include the costs associated with the up-front needs assessment and the evaluation processes.

Cost-Benefit Analysis Approach

The cost-benefit analysis looks at the total cost to produce a training program. This includes everything from the needs assessment, through design, development, delivery, and follow-up. Both direct and indirect costs are used to determine the total cost of the program. As you can see from table 9-1, the task of determining training costs is not easy.

Table 9-1. Determining Training Costs.

Direct Costs			
	People	**Facilities**	**Materials**
Design and Development	Salaries, benefits, travel for • Course development • Clerical support or Consultant fee and expense or Costs of certifying in-house trainer for purchased programs		Marketing brochures Participant materials Instructor manual Purchased resource materials Purchased program

Delivery	Salaries, benefits, travel for	Room rental	Notebooks
	• Trainer(s)	Equipment rental	Folders
	• Participants (average salary)	Refreshments	Tent cards
			Paper
	• Clerical support		Pencils/pens
	Consultant fees and expenses		Flipcharts
			Handouts
			Film rental/purchase
			Transparencies/slides
			Stationery items
			Certificates
			Books
			Article reprints
Evaluation	Salaries, benefits, travel for		Surveys
	• Training personnel		Questionnaires
	• Participants		
	• Clerical support		
	• Bosses		
	• Subordinates		
	• Peers		

Indirect Costs

Training space		Computer time
Custodial services		Equipment depreciation
Utilities		Equipment
Postage		Maintenance/repair
Telephone		Support services

The next step is to determine the total benefits of the program such as reduced costs or increased revenues directly attributable to the training. In many cases, we can only estimate the benefits.

You then subtract the total costs from the total benefits to yield the net benefit of the training program. The program is considered a financial success if the costs are lower than the benefits.

Intangible Benefits

With a program as complex as leadership development, don't overlook the importance of intangible benefits such as increased job satisfaction, improved team work, and increased organization commitment. Make every effort to convert all data into monetary value with the understanding that some soft data cannot be converted. If that is the case, the intangible benefits should still be included with an explanation.

The formulas for calculating the benefit-cost ratio (BCR) and the ROI are as follows:

$$BCR = \frac{\text{Program Benefits}}{\text{Program Costs}}$$

$$\text{Net Benefits} = \text{Program Benefits} - \text{Program Costs}$$

$$ROI\ (\%) = \frac{\text{Net Benefits}}{\text{Program Costs}} \times 100$$

Significance of the Evaluation Process

Evaluation is a complex issue. For one thing, many variables enter into the equation. No matter how hard you try to fine-tune the evaluation process, the reality is that effects can only be estimated and economic benefits cannot be calculated precisely. As the role of training continues to change and trainers reposition themselves as performance consultants, there will be more pressure to measure the effectiveness of training. The good news, however, is that the field of training and development continues to grow at a rapid pace. This trend will continue to provide many opportunities for training professionals, both internal and external, to have an effect on the growth and development of individuals and organizations throughout the world.

 Noted

It is possible that even if a person has learned a skill and applied it on the job, the applied skill may have no effect on the bottom line.

According to Jack Phillips (1998), only programs that meet the following criteria should be selected for ROI analysis:

- ▶ involve a large target audience
- ▶ expect to have a long life cycle
- ▶ are important to strategic objectives
- ▶ link to operational goals and issues
- ▶ are expensive
- ▶ take a significant amount of time
- ▶ have high visibility
- ▶ have a comprehensive needs assessment
- ▶ have the interest of top executives.

Clearly, a comprehensive leadership development program meets these criteria and, therefore, lends itself to an in-depth ROI analysis.

Basic Rule 15

Measurements must be taken at all four levels prior to conducting an ROI evaluation.

Training Results Measurement Model

Another method to evaluate the bottom-line impact of training is the Training Results Measurement (TRM) Model, developed by IBM Learning Services. This approach provides a framework for measuring the bottom-line business value of training and helps bridge the gap between on-the-job application (Level 3) and business results (Level 4). The model uses five interrelated analyses:

- ▶ *Organization Mapping Analysis.* A process that creates a diagram that shows the organization's functions, activities, and processes and their relationship to each other. These include organizational charts, procedure manuals, and process guides.
- ▶ *Performance Measure Analysis.* A process for identifying the performance measures that the organization uses, such as employee opinion surveys, performance appraisals, and business results.

▶ *Causal Chain Analysis*. A process for tracing the impact of leadership development efforts through a chain of organizational measures and linking the program with the desired business results.

▶ *Training Benefit-Cost Analysis*. A process for determining the benefits and the costs of a leadership development program. The benefits may be both qualitative and quantitative.

▶ *Training Investment Analysis*. A process for comparing training benefits and training costs for one or more training investment options. Analytical methods include return-on-investment, internal rate of return, and payback period.

For a complete explanation of the TRM Model, refer to *Infoline*, "Link Training to Your Bottom Line," by Dean Spitzer and Malcolm Conway (2002).

Another helpful resource for determining ROI is "How to Solve the ROI Riddle" by Susan Barksdale and Teri Lund (2003) in *The 2003 Team and Organization Development Sourcebook*.

All three approaches stress the importance of planning for the evaluation and measurement up front before the program is developed. They also affirm that training must be driven by business results.

Getting It Done

Before attempting a Level 5 (ROI) evaluation for the entire leadership development program, start with one small element to increase your comfort level with the process. For example, select a one-day training program and take it through all five levels of evaluation. Then, as your leadership development program grows, you can apply the complete evaluation process to the entire program.

In the final chapter, you will learn some quick tips for developing and implementing a successful leadership development program.

10

Conclusion

■ ■

From reading this book, you have discovered that leadership development is a complex, slow, and ongoing process. Yet the very survival of an organization depends on its commitment and ability to develop leaders at all levels.

Although formal training programs will continue as the core of a leadership development program, more leadership development occurs (and will continue to occur) within the context of work. As part of that context, top leaders, including CEOs, are taking active roles in developing the next generation of leaders. Furthermore, organizations must develop leadership competencies that are in alignment with the business strategy and goals. At the same time, development plans and their associated activities and experiences must be customized to meet the specific needs of the individual as well as those of the organization.

The following tips will serve you well in developing a successful leadership development program that adds value to the organization and truly makes a difference:

- All elements of the program must be linked to business goals and strategies.
- There must be clearly defined, behavior-based leadership competencies.
- The program must have not only top management support but also an internal champion and advocate.
- Everyone in the organization must view the program and process as an investment in the business.

▶ Development plans and the associated experiences must be highly customized and individualized.
▶ The program must be carefully monitored and evaluated by top management.

The result is an integrated, comprehensive leadership development program designed to grow great leaders to outperform the competition and to achieve organizational goals—the real bottom line.

References

Barksdale, S., and T. Lund. "How to Solve the ROI Riddle." *The 2003 Team and Organization Development Sourcebook*, M. Silberman, editor. Alexandria, VA: ASTD Press, 2003.

Betof, E. Interview, March 24, 2008.

Billhardt, B. "Playing Games with Leadership: How Business Simulations and Games Are Growing Tomorrow's Leaders." Accessed April 7, 2008, from www.enspire.com.

Colvin, G. "Leader Machines." *Fortune*, volume 156, number 7, October 1, 2007.

Kaye, B., and D. Scheef. "Mentoring." *Infoline*, April 2000, Issue 0004. Alexandria, VA: ASTD Press.

Kirkpatrick, D.L. "The Four Levels of Evaluation." *Infoline*, January 2007, Issue 0701. Alexandria, VA: ASTD Press.

Lawson, K. *The Trainer's Handbook* (2nd edition). San Francisco: Pfeiffer, 2006.

Leonard, D., and W.C. Swap. *Deep Smarts: How to Cultivate and Transfer Enduring Business Wisdom*. Cambridge, MA: Harvard Business School Press, 2005.

Phillips, J. "Level 5 Evaluation: ROI." *Infoline*, May 1998, Issue 9805. Alexandria, VA: ASTD Press.

Snipes, J. "Identifying and Cultivating High-Potential Employees." *CLO*, October 2005.

Spitzer, D., and M. Conway. "Link Training to Your Bottom Line." *Infoline*, January 2002, Issue 0201. Alexandria, VA: ASTD Press.

Thomas, D.C., and K. Inkson. *Cultural Intelligence*. San Francisco: Berrett-Kohler Publishers, 2003.

Thomas, S.J., and P.J. Douglas. "Structured Mentoring: A New Approach that Works." *Infoline*, January 2004, Issue 0401. Alexandria, VA: ASTD Press.

About the Author

▪▪

Karen Lawson is an international consultant, professional speaker, executive coach, and author. As founder and president of Lawson Consulting Group, she has built a successful consulting firm specializing in organization and management development as well as executive coaching.

Lawson is the author of 10 books on training, communication, leadership, and coaching. She has also written chapters for 20 professional anthologies in addition to numerous articles in professional journals.

She holds a doctorate in adult and organization development from Temple University, an MA from the University of Akron, and a BA from Mount Union College. As of 2008, she is one of only 400 people worldwide to have earned the Certified Speaking Professional designation from the 4,000-member National Speakers Association. She has received numerous awards for her outstanding contribution to the training and speaking professions and was also named one of Pennsylvania's 2005 Best 50 Women in Business and one of the Philadelphia area's Women of Distinction for 2007.

She has been actively involved in professional organizations such as the National Speakers Association and the American Society for Training & Development, holding leadership positions at both the local and national levels.

Lawson is currently an adjunct professor at Arcadia University in the international MBA program and has served on the adjunct faculty of a number of colleges and universities. For more information or to contact Karen Lawson, go to www.LawsonCG.com or email klawson@LawsonCG.com.

Index